Brent Crude Oil

"In this fascinating book, Adi managed to gather a team of experienced 'old hands' who participated in creation and development of the Brent market. Their chapters are a great read and offer lessons for the further development of this most important oil benchmark in the world."
—Pierre Andurand, *Chief Investment Officer, Andurand Capital, UK*

"The book offers a unique insight into the origins of the Brent market and its evolution over the years. It is an essential reference for anyone interested in a deeper understanding of the process of oil price formation and the links between the various Brent layers."
—Dr. Bassam Fattouh, *Director of the Oxford Institute for Energy Studies, UK*

"A fascinating read and a reminder that even the most important markets in the world are created by and sustained by the interplay between people, many larger-than-life. Adi should be congratulated for bringing this story together before it is covered up by the sands of time."
—Paul Horsnell, *Head of Commodities Research at Standard Chartered Bank, and co-author of the seminal book on* Brent: 'Oil Markets and Prices'

"With the help of expert contributors, this book tells the story of the 40+ year journey of Brent and how it remains so important despite numerous challenges. It is a book which is required reading for those of us who worked in or with the Oil & Gas Trading industry, to anyone who wants to understand how a commodity benchmark is formed and maintained, and to anyone who uses energy and would like to understand the effect of Brent on their daily lives."
—Mark Quartermain *(former VP, Crude Oil Trading & Supply for Shell and co-founder of 'Twenty Plus Ten' Board & Executive Advisers)*

"This book provides a comprehensive, rigorous, and fact-based analysis of the history and possible future evolution of Brent on the global scene. It is written by high caliber experts who each have a few decades of operating experience in oil trading and who provide a very authoritative insider view of the functioning and outlook for the "new" Brent oil benchmark. It is a cracking read, and a must for anyone interested in international oil trading."
—Prof. Manfred Hafner, *Adjunct Professor of international energy, The Johns Hopkins University School of Advanced International Studies (SAIS-Europe), Italy and SciencesPo Paris School of International Affairs (PSIA), France*

"This is an important book. Dr. Imsirovic has put together a unique set of contributors to tell the history of the Brent benchmark and its makers. As the world seems poised to once again recalibrate the world oil pricing system, the chapters offer timely historical guidance on what enabled the North Sea oil market to flourish. Combining keen general observations with beautiful personal recollections drawn from ex-traders, this volume should become required reading for anyone interested in understanding how Brent came to be the world's most important price."

—Dr. Jack Seddon, *Associate Professor of International Political Economy in the Faculty of Political Science and Economics at Waseda University, Japan*

Adi Imsirovic
Editor

Brent Crude Oil

Genesis and Development of the World's Most
Important Oil Benchmark

Editor
Adi Imsirovic
Oxford Institute for Energy Studies
Oxford, UK

ISBN 978-3-031-28231-7   ISBN 978-3-031-28232-4   (eBook)
https://doi.org/10.1007/978-3-031-28232-4

Cover illustration: © Melisa Hasan

This Palgrave Macmillan imprint is published by the registered company Springer Nature Switzerland AG
The registered company address is: Gewerbestrasse 11, 6330 Cham, Switzerland

CONTENTS

Notes on Contributors

Adrian Binks is chairman, Chief Executive Officer, and major shareholder of the Argus Media group of companies. He developed the company after buying a partnership in an industry newsletter Europ-Oil Prices and the associated Argus Telex in 1984.

In the same year he took management control, renamed the company, and started the development of a global business under the Argus brand. Argus now has almost 1300 full time staff covering nearly all the major commodity markets including many of the transition fuels to get to net zero. Staff are based in 29 key locations around the world.

Adrian began his career at BP, working in the Public Affairs team and then the Supply and Trading group.

Adrian grew up in Leeds where he attended the local grammar school before studying history at Cambridge University. He won the prestigious EY International Entrepreneur of the Year Award for 2017.

Liz Bossley is the CEO of the Consilience Energy Advisory Group Ltd. From 1978 to 1985 she worked for the UK state oil company, BNOC, then became head of trading and shipping operations for Enterprise Oil.

She set up Consilience in 1999 advising companies on trading and refining issues and acting regularly in disputes as an expert witness. In 2022 she designed 'Revenue Analysis Apportionment and Hedging', an APP designed to help oil producers and asset traders decide how much oil to hedge.

Colin Bryce began his career in Oil Trading and Supply in 1978 with the British National Oil Corporation (BNOC) and Britoil. He joined Morgan Stanley in 1987 to help set up their Oil Trading business outside of the USA.

He has subsequently held positions at Morgan Stanley as Co-Head of Global Commodities, Head of EMEA Institutional Sales and Trading (Equities, Fixed Income, and Commodities), and Chairman of Morgan Stanley Bank International Ltd. He served for 19 years on the board of Morgan Stanley & Co Ltd and was a member of the firm's global management committee.

He is a founding partner of energy consultant Energex.Partners.

Kurt Chapman was a Brent crude oil trader for 29 years, retiring in 2018. In his last position, he managed the international crude oil business for Mercuria, one of the world's largest energy and commodity trading companies, based in Geneva. Prior to Mercuria, he worked for several other prominent companies including Sempra Energy Trading, Koch Supply and Trading, Ashland Oil, and Elf (now Total) Trading. Kurt began his career in 1989 at Morgan Stanley, New York, after serving on active duty as an infantry officer in the United States Marine Corps. He graduated from Harvard University in 1985 with a degree in economics.

Kurt Chapman currently serves as an independent director of Zenith Energy, a midstream company operating bulk liquid storage terminals in the Americas and Europe. With Adi Imsirovic, he has published several papers on the upcoming changes to the Brent benchmark for the Oxford Institute of Energy Studies. Mr. Chapman also dictated a chapter in Owain Johnson's book *40 Classic Crude Oil Trades*. He resides in London.

Neil Fleming is the Senior Vice President, Editorial, at Argus Media, one of the world's largest publishers of market information for the global commodities and energy industries. He manages 530 reporters around the globe, who gather news, report prices, and write analysis about markets in oil, gas, power, emissions, carbon offsets, hydrogen, biofuels, LPG, chemicals, metals, coal, fertilizers, and agriculture.

A journalist and writer for the past 38 years, he has worked across Africa, the Middle East, and the UK, covering wars, famines, wildlife, politics, sport, OPEC, and the international energy industry. He was East Africa and then southern Africa bureau chief for United Press International, before specialising in the politics of OPEC and the Middle East in the early 1990s. From 1997 to 2002 he was editorial head of S&P Global Platts, and from 2009 to 2018 was Strategic Advisor to ICIS, part of RELX. He joined Argus in 2020.

David Godfrey entered the oil industry in 1966 joining Iranian Oil Participants (IOP), a consortium of Western Oil companies. after the demise of IOP after the fall of Shah in 1979, David joined the newly formed British National Oil Corp (BNOC) and became general manager operations. Following the closure of BNOC in 1985 he was recruited by Elf to help set Elf trading S.A. in Geneva as Global Operations manager. In 1999 Elf merged with Total and ETSA became Totsa. David retired but continues to act as a part time consultant helping to digitise trade documentation with ICE.

Nigel Harris was a BP Crude Oil trader until the mid-1980s, when he became one of the most active and well-respected brokers in the market, working with First National, Amerex and Tullet Prebon. He was a senior oil Consultant for Consilience before he retired in 2013.

Adi Imsirovic is a Senior Research Fellow at the Oxford Institute for Energy Studies (OIES) and a director of Surrey Clean Energy, an energy consultancy. Adi has over 35 years of experience in the energy markets, most of it as an oil trader, working in a number of companies at very senior positions such as a Head of Oil Trading (Europe) for Texaco in London, Regional Trading Manager for Texaco in Asia (based in Singapore), and a Global Head of Oil Trading at Gazprom Marketing & Trading in London.

Adi is a Fulbright Scholar and studied at the Graduate School of Arts and Sciences, Harvard University. Adi has a Ph.D. in Economics and a master's degree in Energy Economics. For a number of years, he taught Energy Economics as well as Resource and Environmental Economics at Surrey University.

Adi has written a number of papers and articles on the topic of oil and gas prices, benchmarks, energy security, energy policy, and energy transition. Adi Imsirovic is the author of the book: *Trading and Price Discovery for Crude Oils: Growth and Development of International Oil Markets*, published by Palgrave in August 2021.

David Peniket is Chair of ICE Futures US, Intercontinental Exchange's US-based derivatives market. He is a Director of Qomply Ltd and a member of the Advisory Board of Prism LLP. He served as President of ICE Futures Europe from 2006 to 2017. David joined the International Petroleum Exchange as Head of Finance in January 1999, prior to its acquisition by Intercontinental Exchange in 2001. He previously spent seven years with KPMG, where he trained as an accountant. He is a trustee of Wesley House, the Methodist College in Cambridge.

CHAPTER 1

Introduction

Adi Imsirovic

Abstract Brent benchmark is perhaps the most complex benchmark in the world. With the inclusion of WTI Midland (from June 2023), it will become even more so. But the options for boosting the volume of oil in the contract were limited. In order to discuss the future of the benchmark, we first must study its past and draw lessons from history.

Keywords Benchmarks · WTI · Brent

COMPLEXITY OF BRENT

The Brent market has always presented the observer with an enigma: unwieldy, archaic and complicated, yet the most important commodity market in the world.

A. Imsirovic (✉)
Oxford Institute for Energy Studies, Ascot, UK
e-mail: adi.imsirovic@surreyenergy.uk

1

Brent has its forward and futures markets, partials, CFDs, EFPs and DFLs, EFS, TAS and many indices. Its price is assessed with the help of derivatives markets as well as with the help of FAF, sulphur, quality adjustments and many other methods that are often unfathomable to a newcomer to this benchmark.[1]

But since 1990s, Brent has had serious problems, caused by falling volumes of oil available for the price assessment. Following an alleged squeeze early in 2000, efforts were made to increase the number of cargoes eligible for the price assessment of Brent. This was done by including ship-to-ship transfers, widening the nomination 'window' and introducing new grades of North Sea oil into the pool of crudes that can be delivered into the Brent contract.[2]

Such efforts brought increasing complexity in the benchmark. Inclusion of new grades required sulphur, quality and freight adjustments. Rules governing the eligibility of bids, offers and trades have been tightened over time and electronic trading platforms introduced to facilitate the assessment process.[3] As we write this, only two or three cargoes of Brent are loaded at the Sullom Voe terminal in the Shetland Islands each month. What has remained of Brent is just the brand name for the benchmark of incredible complexity. Yet, with the falling North Sea production of oil, liquidity problems continued. With volume of 'Brent' falling to some 700,000 barrels in 2022, something urgent needed to be done to save the benchmark.

Two solutions were on offer.[4] One option was inclusion of a relatively new and prolific Norwegian stream of Johan Sverdrup crude into the Brent 'basket'.[5] But this solution had two problems: the grade was heavy and had a high sulphur content, very different from the 'sweet' grades of oil already in the Brent basket. Secondly, Johan Sverdrup was operated and largely controlled by Equinor, a company already dominating other three grades eligible for assessment in the Brent benchmarks—Oseberg, Ekofisk and Troll. This market concentration was a problem for many players in the market, and the majority of the market participants[6] opted for another solution.[7]

After further consultations, on the 8th of June 2022, Platts, a price reporting agency (PRA) and a part of 'S&P Global Commodity Insights', announced that it would include West Texas Intermediate (WTI) Midland crude oil in its Dated Brent benchmark, with effect from June 2023.[8]

The most complex commodity benchmark just became even more complicated. Liz Bossley, the author of Chapter 3 in this book, commented that: 'Brent was barely held together by duct tape'.

Despite such an appearance, the inclusion of another major and rival oil benchmark is not just a patch. It may bring a radical change. With volumes of the North Sea production falling and United States (US) production growing, there is a chance that the Brent benchmark may well be dominated and probably entirely swamped by WTI. If that is the case, why would the market bother with Brent at all? Why not just use the WTI benchmark instead?

But during the COVID-19 pandemic, WTI had its fair share of problems, trading at a significantly negative price at one stage, while the Brent complex coped relatively well with the increased volatility.[9] So, the debate on this subject continues.

Economic History as a Guide

Having observed and taken part in this debate over the future of Brent, it became increasingly obvious to me that the history of the origins and development of the Brent market was the most important guide in discussing its future development. Yet, there has been relatively little recorded economic history of the Brent market.

Two seminal works have been written about Brent: 'The Market for North Sea Crude Oil' by Mabro et al. (1986) and 'Oil Markets and Prices' by Horsnell and Mabro (1993). But these were indepth studies of the functioning of the Brent market and not economic histories of its development. In particular, the individuals shaping the genesis and development of the world's most important oil benchmark have barely been mentioned. This became very obvious to me when researching my book on 'Trading and Price Discovery for Crude Oils'. I spent many hours interviewing various participants in the oil markets, but the scope of my book simply did not allow for more detailed accounts of many of the events concerning the Brent market.[10]

The purpose of this book is to fill in that gap. And who better to write about it than the participants in the early days of the Brent market themselves? Early in 2022, I floated the idea about such a book with Liz Bossley and Colin Bryce, doyens of the oil industry—and they were very positive about it. Another colleague, Kurt Chapman had already written a lengthy piece on the legacy of Brent which I peer-reviewed a year or two previously. It needed more work and I suggested that he turned it into a chapter in the book, and he agreed. From there, the idea snowballed, as all the eventual authors shared our enthusiasm and a belief that such a book simply had to be written.

There were several constraints, however. First, there was a time constraint. I wanted the publication of the book to coincide with the launch of the 'new Brent' contract, in June 2023. The second one was concerning the authors. I approached as many of the key players in the early days of the Brent market as I could get in touch with. Some of them politely declined because they did not want to talk about the past events, some were not happy to write lengthy pieces, others were not granted a permission from their employer (especially when the employer was the government) and sadly, a few were unwell or simply not around anymore. The latter factor confirmed my urgency to complete this project. To meet our deadline, Palgrave decided to print the book in their 'Pivot' edition, which put a limit on the length of the book.[11]

The Layout of the Book

The book begins with a brief history of the oil markets explaining how and why we came to use benchmarks such as Brent in oil transactions. The main message of this chapter is that the natural state of the oil market is competition, and oligopolistic structures that have dominated it for many decades are the result of either government inaction to regulate market power or a very deliberate government policy to create national champions, often with wider geopolitical agendas. Even competitive markets need government support and protection, achieved by providing solid legal and regulatory framework and removing obstacles to free trade.

In Chapter 3, Liz Bossley explains the origins of the Brent market. In all energy markets, policy plays an essential role, and the Brent market is no exception. Following the early discoveries of oil and gas in the UK sector of the North Sea, the Labour government of Harold Wilson enacted The Petroleum and Submarine Pipeline Act which established the British National Oil Corporation ('BNOC'), the British state oil champion. Originally working as an oil trader at BNOC, Ms. Bossley is perfectly positioned to explain the role of the government policy and taxation on the genesis of the Brent market.

While the BNOC's involvement in 15-day Brent market encouraged its growth, it was also recognised that the market could be a perfect tool for minimising taxation for the larger players in the North Sea oil industry. So called 'tax spinning' is explained in detail in this chapter. Nigel Harris, one of the well-respected brokers in the market at the time, explains the role of brokers in facilitating such 'spinning' activity: '*Love 'em or hate 'em,* He says, '*brokers were a major contributor to the liquidity of the 15-day Brent market in the 1980s and remain so today for the markets that have subsequently evolved*'.

In Chapter 4, Colin Bryce, a BNOC oil trader, turned a successful 'Wall Street refiner', takes up the story to show how the fiscal regime and liberalisation policies in the 1980s made '... *the senior executives of big oil realise that there was a whole new revenue stream to be captured by speculating in oil markets... The independent trade houses flocking to the honeypot were paying big salaries and the oil company "bench traders" were in great demand. Everyone wanted the boom to continue and, indeed, to expand*'.

This chapter covers the development of the whole ecosystem of players in the Brent market in rich detail. Many of the players at the time, such as the Japanese Sogo Shoshas and traders such as Trans World Oil (TWO), Marc Rich, Bomar, Sirco, Gotco, Carey, Tradax and many others (with backing of some very colourful individuals such as John Deuss, supposedly seen by some in the market as a mysterious Bond-like figure; smart, gregarious and well-connected Nancy Kropp, and families such as Hindujas and Rothschilds) have long since left the market.

But what has remained is a rich record of how various players, and banks in particular, contributed to the price discovery and risk management using swaps, options and other derivative instruments from the financial markets. Eventually, one such 'partials Brent' market led to the development of the first Brent oil exchange, the International Petroleum Exchange or IPE.

In Chapter 5, Kurt Chapman shares his experience and knowledge of pure crude oil trading. He explores the workings of the evolving Brent complex, identifies inconsistencies between the physical, forward and futures markets and examines different trading strategies.

The chapter describes how traders first optimised operational tolerance driving liquidity in the Brent forward contract. It then explains how dislocations between the different Brent instruments created money making opportunities.

The chapter also discusses the concept of convergence. In February 2015, there was a discrepancy between the Brent forward contract, which moved to a month ahead (30-day) nomination period while the ICE Brent futures contract remained a 15-day nomination. This resulted in fewer cargoes available to determine the Brent index, creating further trading opportunity.

Mr. Chapman describes a real-life example of time arbitrage. Utilising forward and futures markets as well as Dated Brent swaps, his company managed a large storage position in Saldanha Bay, South Africa. While readers not well versed in trading may find this chapter a challenging read, it gives us a fascinating insight into the mind of one of the industry's legendary Brent traders.

Chapter 6 was written by one of the most experienced Brent operators in the business, David Godfrey. He was a manager of crude oil operations for BNOC before moving on to a newly formed trading arm of Elf Trading S.A. in Geneva (now TotalEnergies Trading and Shipping), one of the key players in the Brent markets. He explains why the Brent operations are very different from the operations of other oil contracts. The nomination procedure, from seller to the buyer and with a sharp deadline for passing the nominations at five a clock London time, created such pressures on the operators that multiple phone lines and atomic clocks were used to avoid the infamous 'clocking', a situation in which a nomination could not be passed on to another buyer and large financial loss was almost guaranteed. With each physical Brent cargo trading many times, the resulting 'daisy chains' created headaches for the operators as the full set of documents, issued once the physical cargo has loaded took many months and even years to through the trade chain (including banks) to reach the end receiver. This resulted in extensive use of the letters of indemnity (LOIs), which unfortunately, could lead to lengthy and costly legal actions (mostly settled out of court). For this reason, David has been one of the earliest proponents of electronic documentation such as bills of lading.

In Chapter 7, former President of ICE Futures Europe, David Peniket revisits the early years of the International Petroleum Exchange (IPE) and the turbulent years of transition of the exchange from the open outcry trading in the pits to the electronic trading platform we know today. David describes the attempt to establish a Brent futures contract based on a physical delivery of crude in tank in Rotterdam. Eventually, it succeeded with a contract mimicking the existing, forward Brent contract with a delivery (free on board or FOB) on a vessel at the Sullom Voe terminal.

The contract was financially settled (with no physical delivery), using a 'Brent Index',[12] an important feature of the Brent futures contract today.

It is a fascinating story of how a small, electronic platform eventually bought a major oil exchange. Electronic trading had solid support from some of the biggest names and liquidity providers in oil trading: BP, Shell, Total, Goldman Sachs and Morgan Stanley. In return, investing in the exchange was probably the most profitable venture they ever made. It is also a story of how the selfish interest of a few entrenched incumbents, supporting the old, open outcry trading method can backfire spectacularly. This is a great lesson for some current incumbents who have similarly been holding back progress in global metal trading.[13]

It is hard to separate the history of oil trading from the history of Price Reporting Agencies (PRAs). Chapter 8 is a story of the pivotal role that the PRAs have played in the price discovery for crude oil and therefore oil trading. The authors of the chapter are two key people in their business: Adrian Binks has been the Chief Executive of the Argus Media group since 1984. Neil Fleming works for Adrian as global head of Editorial at Argus.

Before anyone accuses the book of being biased towards one of the two biggest PRAs in the world, I must mention that I approached Platts at a very senior level about recommending someone I would talk to about the early days of Brent. To my surprise, they recommended Neil Fleming! This is because during the 1997–2002 period, Neil ran the global editorial and data group at S&P Global Platts, and first worked for Platts in the mid-1980s. Further, from 2009 to 2018, he was Strategic Advisor to ICIS, another large PRA, and also managed its editorial operations for a year. Adrian and Neil explain how the price assessment process evolved together with the changing market. By 'holding up a mirror to the market, in their unique independent and competitive position as benchmark providers, PRAs can also usher in change'.

The last chapter sums up the arguments in this book and, in the light of the economic history learned from the authors, offers an insight into the future of the benchmark. Brent may well be becoming terribly complex, but as Joe Roeber, a keen observer, and a consultant to the oil industry during the formation of traded markets in the 1970s and 1980s noticed:

It may appear to be a paradox that Brent prices are allowed to have such importance when the market itself is so ramshackle in its operation and subject to powerful extra-economic pressures, such as tax and speculation. But this is only a paradox if tidiness per se is an economic virtue.[14]

The Brent market naturally evolved over time and its complexity and even some redundancies are natural features, not dissimilar from the features of the human body—they are not always pretty or perfect, but they work well.

All of the chapters in this book have an overlap of topics. But the idea is that the overlapping topics are seen from very different viewpoints, hopefully providing the full picture of the development of Brent.

THE MISSION

This book could have been much bigger. Having finished the manuscript, I have been approached by several market participants who expressed their interest in adding to the existing material. It is not inconceivable that, at some stage, the book is expanded. In the meantime, I hope that the existing chapters encourage some of the authors to think about expanding them into their own, full-blown books. Most of them certainly have enough material to do so, as the hardest part of editing this monograph has been keeping the word count within the agreed limits.

In spite of these constraints, I am sure that this effort will make a contribution to the economic history of oil markets. The hope is that it will find a wide readership: From researchers to young people learning about the commodity markets to the policy makers increasingly supervising markets. At a deeper level, it will contribute the understanding of what makes markets develop and grow, and how to avoid the mistakes of the past in managing the markets of the future.

This is one of the key purposes of the book. We have entered the age of the energy transition and markets have a very important role to play in this transition. Yet, there is plenty of evidence that government intervention in the perfectly functioning markets is becoming the norm, slowing the pace of transition to cleaner future. For example, COP26 in Glasgow agreed to phase out subsidies for fossil fuels,[15] yet a year later, those subsidies more than doubled.[16] A belief that markets can somehow be manipulated for 'greater good' is misplaced. It originates in the lack of understanding of how markets work and evolve. Let's hope that this book can make a contribution towards remedying that problem.

NOTES

1. Brent partials usually trade as 100,000-barrel part-cargoes in the physical, forward market. Contracts for Difference or CFDs are swaps between Dated Brent and forward Brent prices (usually traded on weekly basis). Dated to Front Line or DFLs are swaps between Dated Brent and the futures front month Brent settlements (usually on monthly basis). Exchange of Futures for Swaps are derivatives linking swaps, usually Dubai, usually on monthly basis with futures markets (usually Brent). Brent index is the price at which the futures market contract expires at the end of the month. Brent can be Traded At Settlement (TAS). The assessment for Dated Brent is made using the forward dated Brent curve, constructed using the observed CFD trades. Freight Adjustment Factor or FAF is used to adjust all the freight costs to a common denominator. Sulphur and quality adjustments are made to reduce the discounts or premiums of grades in the Brent 'basket' (Brent, Forties, Oseberg, Ekofisk and Troll—BFOET or often BFOE for short) for an easier comparison—a handicap system of sorts.

   For more details, see Fattouh and Imsirovic (June 2019).
2. See Imsirovic (2021, Chapter 11).
3. Ibid., 'The Early Brent Assessments', page 162. Also see Chapter 5 of this book by K. Chapman.
4. For details, See Imsirovic and Chapman (March 2022).
5. Currently, grades of oil eligible for delivery into the Brent contract are Brent, Forties, Oseberg, Ekofisk and Troll.
6. This was done on the basis of market consultations between the PRAs and traders involved in the market.
7. See Imsirovic and Chapman (March 2022).
8. On January 31, 2023, Platts also confirmed the inclusion of WTI Midland into the assessment of the forward Brent contract. See: https://www.spglobal.com/commodityinsights/en/our-methodology/subscriber-notes/013123-platts-confirms-inclusion-of-wti-midland-in-cash-bfoe-from-june-2023-contract-month-adds-further-guidance.
9. See Imsirovic (2021, Chapter 13, page 196 and Chapter 15).
10. There were minor exceptions such as the interview with Jorge Montepeque. Ibid., page 162.
11. Maximum length of a Pivot edition is 50,000 words.
12. https://www.theice.com/futures-europe/brent.
13. 'The London Metal Exchange has just seen over 90 days of turbulence, arguably the worst in the history of the 145-year-old trading platform'. https://www.fnlondon.com/articles/london-metal-exchanges-tumultuous-three-months-heres-what-happened-20220610.

14. I am grateful to Colin Bryce for pointing out this quotation. Joe Roeber (1993, page 44).
15. https://www.newscientist.com/article/2297452-cop26-world-agrees-to-phase-out-fossil-fuel-subsidies-and-reduce-coal/.
16. This was a direct result of government price controls, caps and subsidies. See: https://www.iea.org/reports/fossil-fuels-consumption-subsidies-2022.

REFERENCES

Fattouh and Imsirovic (June 2019): 'Contracts for Difference and the Evolution of the Brent Complex', Oxford Energy Comment.

Horsnell, P., and Mabro, R. (1993): *Oil Markets and Prices*, Oxford University Press.

Imsirovic, A. (2019): *Changes to the 'Dated Brent' Benchmark: More to Come*, Oxford Energy Comment, March 2019.

Imsirovic, A. (2021): 'Trading and Price Discovery for Crude Oils', Palgrave.

Imsirovic, A., and Chapman, K. (March 2022): 'The Future of the Brent Oil Benchmark A Radical Makeover', Oxford Energy Comment.

Mabro, R., Bacon, R., Chadwick, M., Halliwell, M., and Long, D. (1986): *The Market for North Sea Crude Oil*, Oxford University Press for the Oxford Institute for Energy Studies.

Roeber, Joe. (1993): 'The Evolution of Oil Markets', The Royal Institute of International Affairs.

CHAPTER 2

The Age of Oil Benchmarks

Adi Imsirovic

Abstract The natural state of the oil market is competition, and oligopolistic structures that have dominated it for many decades are the result of either government inaction to regulate market power or a very deliberate government policy to create national champions, often with wider geopolitical agendas. Even competitive markets need government support and protection, achieved by providing solid legal and regulatory framework and removing obstacles to free trade. Since 1980s oil market became fairly competitive again, and we entered the age of benchmarks, in which Brent became the dominant global price of oil.

Keywords Oil oligopoly · Seven Sisters · Oil pricing · Energy policy

A. Imsirovic (✉)
Oxford Institute for Energy Studies, Ascot, UK
e-mail: adi.imsirovic@surreyenergy.uk

© The Author(s), under exclusive license to Springer Nature
Switzerland AG 2023
A. Imsirovic (ed.), *Brent Crude Oil*,
https://doi.org/10.1007/978-3-031-28232-4_2

OPEC PRICING SYSTEM COLLAPSES

The introduction of benchmarking in oil trade started in the 1980s, following a major price collapse and the inability of the Organisation for Petroleum Exporting Countries (OPEC) to control the price of oil. Following the collapse of the defence of the $18 price, personally directed by the Saudi King Fahd,[1] the Aramco partners (Exxon, Mobil, Texaco, and Chevron) refused to lift oil unless they were given lower, market-related prices.[2] Eventually, Aramco reached an agreement with the partner companies to sell its oil based on prices of the internationally traded crude oils: West Texas Intermediate (WTI) for sales to the Americas,[3] North Sea Brent for deliveries to Europe, and average of Oman and Dubai for sales to Asia. The arrangement was made public in January 1988, and the rest of OPEC soon adopted it.

This is pretty much the basis on which oil is trading today.

The shift to market-related prices did not mean that the market was going back to the early days of the competitive oil industry of 1860s and 1870s in Pennsylvania. OPEC remained the proverbial 'elephant in the room', continuing to play a significant role in the market. Over time, OPEC tried and tested various policies to keep market prices well above their cost of production, thus maximising its revenues. However, the price of oil was being set by an increasingly large number of diverse players, including traders, hedgers, investment funds, and speculators, making it harder for any group of players to dominate the price-making process.

The international oil market took some time to develop. A number of factors came into play to facilitate its development. High oil prices and diversification of risk by major oil companies incentivised exploration of new regions of the world. Production picked up significantly in Alaska, Mexico, Russia, and the North Sea. With the vertically integrated systems of the oil majors broken, these new volumes of oil were spilling over into the marketplace, revealing the real market transactions, and prices. But having the old trade channels broken and excess oil looking for alternative buyers was not sufficient for the market to grow. The key additional ingredient was the government policy.

As we are going to show in this book, Brent emerged as a premier international oil benchmark with the help of the UK's fiscal treatment of the North Sea oil production and the liberalisation policies of the government of Margaret Thatcher in 1980s.

In order to fully understand the reasons for the emergence of Brent and other benchmarks, it is important to revisit the key historical events that led to it. That knowledge can help us understand that well-functioning markets cannot be left to themselves and that governments play a critical role in regulating monopolies and promoting competition.

Markets, Market Power, and Monopolies in the Oil Market

Oil markets are prone to concentration of market power. However, the best examples of monopoly power in the oil markets have not only been a result of poor government regulation of the markets but were often a result of the government encouragement to concentrate market power.

The most successful concentration of market power in the oil market, and probably any global commodity market, was the oligopoly of seven international major oil companies or 'Seven Sisters'.[4] Their story begun with a conference arranged by the British Foreign Office in March 1914. In this meeting, the British and German governments muscled into a foreign company, 'Turkish Petroleum Company', a brainchild of one shrewd Armenian, Calouste Gulbenkian, and a Turkish sultan Abdul Hamid.[5]

At the turn of the century, the most promising, oil-rich regions of Mesopotamia were under Turkish control. On Gulbenkian's advice, the sultan transferred the most promising acreage into his personal possession and approved a concession to be held by the Turkish Petroleum Company (TPC, eventually to become the Iraq Petroleum Company or IPC). Half of the company shareholding was owned by the Central Bank of Turkey (including Gulbenkian's share and a British syndicate, led by D'Arcy, the founder of Anglo-Iranian) and the rest equally owned by a subsidiary of Royal Dutch Shell and Deutsche Bank. After the First World War, the German interests were given to the French government, following the San Remo agreement in April 1920.

A few years before, the government of Britain made another well-timed decision. Only two weeks after the British parliament passed a resolution to buy a controlling share in the Anglo-Persian Oil Company in June 1914, Archduke Franz Ferdinand was assassinated in Sarajevo. Within weeks, The Great War started.

The British government involvement in the Middle East exploration angered the American allies, who saw it as imperial and discriminatory.

After the war, Americans saw the world through an equal, non-exclusive, and competitive, 'open door' lens. At least until they got in. Following the British, the US State Department started actively supporting the American oil companies in the region and pushed for negotiations to obtain a share of the TPC. Eventually, after six years of difficult negotiations, the 'Red Line Agreement'[6] was finally signed in the summer of 1928. The American companies secured an equal (23.75%) share, the same as the British, French, and Royal Dutch Shell interests. Having argued for an 'open door' policy for almost a decade, and having obtained a fair share, the American oil companies happily helped firmly shut it.

The concentration of market power was actively encouraged by the participating governments. This was particularly true after the Second World War from which the old colonial powers emerged economically weak, encouraging the US policymakers to expand its strategic and commercial interests to secure a dominant role in the Middle East.

The Bahrain concession was developed in 1932 by the Standard Oil of California[7] (now Chevron) with some strong 'arm-twisting' from the US Department of State.[8] It was followed by major finds in Saudi Arabia, where the legendary Max Steineke, a Standard California geologist discovered Abqaiq field in 1938, followed by Ghawar in 1948, the largest oil field in the world.[9] There, Standard California and Texaco, together with Standard of New Jersey (later Exxon) and Socony (later Mobil), jointly set up the Arabian American Oil Company (ARAMCO) as well as the Trans-Arabian Pipeline Company (TAPCO). In Kuwait, the concession was controlled by Gulf Oil (later also Mobil) and Anglo-Iranian (later BP). In Qatar, the partners were the same as in the IPC (Iraq), and so on.

The mechanisms for controlling these large petroleum reserves were ingenious, generally based on various common 'rules' such as Average Program Quantity (APQ) in Iran, the 'Five Sevenths' rule in Iraq and the 'Dividend Squeeze' in Saudi Arabia.[10] In a nutshell, these and other rules were designed to restrict the production to the level that balances the actual demand, so the crude oil ends up in the integrated systems of the major oil companies, with a minimal effect on markets and prices. The companies avoided competition, especially in the Far East, where most of the Middle East oil was marketed. The arrangements made sure there was no competition, no markets, and no price for crude oil in the region, other than what the majors decided it to be.

After the war, the European Recovery Program (ERP) of 1948, popularly known as 'Marshall Plan', was partly designed to cement the dominant position of the US companies in the strategically important Middle East: 'In addition to its profit potential, due to low production costs, the Middle East was the natural supply source to Western Europe and Japan. Control over the region, thus, would give the US influence over the economic and military policies of almost all the major participants in World War II'.[11]

The monopoly of the major oil companies or 'Seven Sisters' can be easily seen through discriminatory pricing for oil produced in the Middle East. It started during the war, in 1944, when the British Auditor General complained about being charged bunker prices for the Royal Navy, based on very high USG prices plus some non-existent 'phantom freight' to the Middle East, for the product refined from cheap Iranian oil in the Abadan refinery.[12] This was due to the price system being based on shipping oil from the US Gulf (USG).[13] This meant that oil and petroleum products sold anywhere else in the world traded at some premium over the USG price (so-called 'US Gulf Plus' pricing), normally equal to the cost of shipping from the Gulf to the point of sale. With the growing importance of oil from the Middle East, where the cost of production was far lower, this difference in cost as well as 'phantom freight' charged by the majors was a source of large profits.[14]

By the 1950s, the seven major oil companies, with the help of their respective governments, achieved global market dominance in all aspects of the oil business. This control was exercised through direct or indirect control of concessions, joint ventures of corporations and their affiliates, long-term contracts, and marketing agreements as well as information sharing, contractual and informal, via interlocking directorships. The companies controlled the largest oil reserves in the world, located in Venezuela, the Persian Gulf, and Indonesia. Oil producing countries needed their expertise and integrated outlets for the oil. They needed the 'Sisters' to fine-tune the supply of oil from various producers to match the overall global demand, without 'disruptive' price competition.

In 1949, the majors controlled 65% of the world reserves (82% of reserves outside the US and 92% outside the US, Russia, and Mexico); produced 95% of oil in the Eastern Hemisphere and 99% of the oil from the Middle East; owned 77% of the global refining capacity outside the US and Russia, as well as two-thirds of the privately owned tanker fleet and pretty much every single, important pipeline outside the US.[15]

Consuming country governments, and the US government in particular, needed the major oil companies not only to keep the supply of oil stable and affordable, but they also used them as an instrument of their foreign policy. Under a real or perceived threat of Communism, the policy started to develop after the war, supporting pro-Western governments through economic growth and a steady, affordable supply of oil. This was to be achieved through a dominant role of the American companies in the world trade. This required the highest level of the state to close ranks with the large oil companies.

Having achieved a full control of the world oil markets, the oil prices 'posted' by the major companies primarily took a role of a taxation instrument on the basis of which the consuming country revenues were based: '… after 1959, no posted price number has any meaning as a price. It can serve only as an interim figure for calculating the per barrel tax'.[16]

There were no real markets, no meaningful prices, and no price volatility to worry about. As long as the posted prices were stable, the producing country governments were assured of stable revenues.

OIL PRODUCERS IN CHARGE

Large profits of monopolists have always attracted newcomers. Smaller, 'independent' oil companies appeared on the scene looking for a piece of the pie. For example, a new round of concessions in Venezuela in 1957 attracted US independents such as Sun, Phillips, and Sinclair which soon produced about 10% of the country's output.[17] In the Middle East, newcomers, such as J.P. Getty paid producing countries more for concessions and offered higher royalties. Despite paying a lot more, Getty still made a fortune.[18]

In Algeria, the French discovered oil in 1957. By the end of the War of Independence in 1962, the country was supplying 40% of all the French oil imports. At the same time in Libya, some sixty concessions were awarded, involving the Oasis Group of US independents, Occidental, Conoco, Bunker Hunt, and others. Most of the Libyan production ended up in the hands of companies that had no integrated systems in Europe and hence no outlets for the oil. Around the same time, BP and Shell found oil in Nigeria, opening West Africa as a new oil frontier. By the end of the 1950s, the USSR became the second-largest producer in the world, after the US, and produced a volume of oil that could compete with the

Middle East. In 1946, nine oil companies operated in the Middle East. By 1970, this number reached 81.[19]

New state-owned refineries, with no integrated supply arrangements, begun to appear on the scene, looking for oil. These were large scale importers in countries such as Italy, Japan, India, Brazil, Argentina, and others. They would tender for the cheapest oil available in the market and often make the awards public, revealing the market conditions and prices.

An oversupplied market, 'leaking' cheap oil trading at prices made public, begun to crumble. Lower spot market prices (Chart 2.1) meant higher discounts relative to the posted prices (used for tax reference), and higher effective tax rate. The majors were losing money, market share, and the ability to balance the market and keep prices stable.

Around the same time, a new breed of populist leaders emerged in some of the producing countries: Gamal Abdel Nasser in Egypt, Muammar al-Qaddafi in Libya, Houari Boumediene in Algiers, Abdullah Tariki in Saudi Arabia, and Perez Alfonso in Venezuela. Apart from being well educated, they shared strong anti-colonial, left-leaning, and nationalist feelings. The Algerian President argued for the producing countries to lead the 'Third World' towards a more equitable and just global world order.

This was a revolutionary period marked by the Suez crisis, anti-colonial movements, Sputnik and the Cuban revolution. The years between 1958

Chart 2.1   Crude oil prices 1950–2019 (*Source* Author and BP Statistical Review)

and 1960 were equally revolutionary in the oil market. In 1958, in Iraq, a group of officers overthrew the British installed monarchy and established a republic. A year later, a revolution in Venezuela removed a military dictator and elected a democratic government. The country increased taxes on the oil industry to almost 70%. The confidence of smaller nations and ex-colonies was growing, and oil prices were falling. The producers were still thinking about oil, but this time collectively.

The key meeting of the oil producing nations was the First Arab Petroleum Congress in Cairo in 1958, and the document that came from the Congress was an unofficial 'understanding' of representatives from S. Arabia, Kuwait, Egypt, Syria, Iran, and Venezuela, the so-called 'Maadi Agreement'.[20] This often neglected but historically important 'pact' stated the aspirations of the producing nations: to increase their share of oil revenues, support prices (on which tax revenues were based), be consulted before any changes are made in posted prices, increase the refining throughput inside the producing countries, establish national oil companies, and coordinate production policies through a commission that was to meet annually. While it had no legal consequence, the 'Maadi Agreement' was a road map for everything the OPEC nations would strive for in the decades to come.

Spot markets continued to trade well below the posted prices, resulting in companies paying effectively higher rates of tax.

The problem was an oil pricing structure that did not make any sense. The Majors were struggling to balance the market by rationing supplies. They simply could not keep prices fixed. Instead, the prices were dictated by the spot market trades.

Under pressure, the majors begun to reduce their posted prices. Most importantly, they did so unilaterally, without any consultation with the producing countries, sovereign states, who were severely impacted by these changes. In other words, the majors were passing the revenue risk on to the producing countries which were unable to manage it. They showed little empathy for their main partners, producing nations. Early in 1959, BP cut postings and got away with it. In August, Jersey Standard (Exxon) announced a further cut in posted prices, but this time there was a strong reaction.

On the very same day, Venezuela banned all the sales of its oil at large discounts. The 'aspirations' of the Maadi Pact turned into action. On the 14th of September 1960, Venezuela, S. Arabia, Iran, Iraq, and Kuwait met in Baghdad and set up the Organisation of the Petroleum Exporting Countries (OPEC). Their agreement was short and to the point:[21]

> *The principal aim of the Organization shall be the unification of petroleum policies for the Member Countries and the determination of the best means for safeguarding the interests of Member Countries individually and collectively.*

The agreement recognised the finite nature of oil and its importance to the development of producing countries, as well as their vulnerability to its price fluctuations. It proposed a unified and opened (to new members) front in formulating production agreements and energy policy in general. It demanded that:

> *'Oil Companies maintain their prices steady and free from all unnecessary fluctuations … to restore present prices to the levels prevailing before the reductions…'* It proposed: *'That Members shall study and formulate a system to ensure the stabilisation of prices by, among other means, the regulation of production…'.*

Finally, it recommended regular consultations and the establishment of the secretariat responsible for the organisation and administration of the organisation.

If the Majors could not stabilise the market, OPEC members believed, their organisation could do it. The very act of setting up OPEC gave them a strong sense of empowerment and control over the most important resource they possessed. One of the signatories of the original Baghdad agreement, and one of the key founding fathers of OPEC, Venezuelan oil minister, Perez Alfonso believed he knew how to do it. A careful student of the US oil industry and the Texas Railroad Commission in particular, he saw it as a blueprint for an OPEC production (quota) rationing system. This view was shared by his 'brother in arms', Saudi oil minister Al-Tariki, who also trained at the Texas Railroad Commission.[22]

It is easy to accuse OPEC of trying to replace one cartel (of international oil majors) with another one (of the oil producing countries), but it is important to realise that anyone living in the decades following the World War 2 did not know anything better than a globally managed oil market.

It took OPEC almost ten years to make any impact on the oil market. It was at the Vienna Conference in June 1968 that a few key principles were adopted in The Declaratory Statement of the Petroleum Policy: Each government was to draw detailed plans for implementing the best conservation practices, producers themselves were to establish basis for the posted prices and most importantly, acquire a maximum degree of participation possible from the oil companies, using the argument of 'changing circumstances'.[23] Fadhil Chalabi, described these principles as '...*the most influential factor in shaping the future of the oil industry and oil policies... reaffirming the right of the OPEC countries to exercise permanent sovereignty over their hydrocarbon resources... was instrumental in heralding a fundamental change in the oil industry and in oil companies' policies*'.

It is hard to disagree with these comments, especially as the section of the Resolution concerning 'Posted Prices or tax reference Prices' clearly and explicitly states that setting these were to pass into the domain of the oil producers: '*Such price shall be determined by the Government and shall move in such a manner as to prevent any deterioration in its relationship to the prices of manufactured goods traded internationally... such price shall be consistent, subject to differences in gravity, quality and geographic location, with the levels of posted or tax reference prices generally prevailing for hydrocarbons in other OPEC Countries and accepted by them as a basis for tax payments*'.[24]

The flip side of the problem with posted prices was when the spot market prices started trading above the posted prices, the producers experienced an effective tax cut. In the early 1970s, this poorly designed system, under the onslaught of genuine post-colonial ambitions, nationalism, rivalry, and war, created a chaotic atmosphere of subsequent declarations, meetings, and agreements, only to be broken months or even days after they were made. Essentially, all the bargaining between the producers and companies were essentially tax revenue negotiations.[25]

The war of 1973 and the oil embargo that followed, accelerated the events which were already under way. On October 16th, at a meeting in Kuwait, OPEC unilaterally increased the price of the main Saudi grade, Arab Light, now the OPEC benchmark crude oil, and proclaimed that the organisation would be the sole arbiter of prices.[26]

Arab Light (with specific gravity of some 34 API and 1.7% sulphur content) sold by Saudi Arabia and well accepted by most refiners around the world became the reference point or benchmark for all the other grades of oil within OPEC. All the other grades of oil with different qualities would adjust their prices to the agreed Arab Light price by applying quality differentials to reflect their relative refining value.

The producers were not just high on confidence, but also awash with oil revenues,[27] enabling them to 'conserve' production if they so wished, but also to acquire the operating company assets. In January, Kuwait followed the Libyan example and acquired 60% of Kuwait Oil Company. Abu Dhabi and Qatar followed, and, by the end of 1974, the Saudis agreed, in principle, to a 100% takeover of Aramco.

But the 1979 Iranian revolution brought yet another bonanza to the producers. With the sudden loss of some five million barrels of Iranian oil, a number of companies who have been producing oil in Iran now effectively became just third-party buyers and had to look for the lost barrels elsewhere. Carefully engineered horizontal and vertical integration of the oil industry by oil majors over decades was broken and oil increasingly traded bilaterally, on cargo-by-cargo basis in the spot markets.

While OPEC effectively took control of the posted prices for oil, it had no mechanism for rationing production to balance the market without the help of oil companies. But it did not seem to matter as long as the oil demand kept growing and prices kept rising. In spite of the agreed posted prices, some producers raised them again unilaterally.[28] OPEC was effectively 'riding' the wave of rising oil prices without having any control over it. But it was not going to last for long.

Spot Markets and the Age of Benchmarks

For oil producers, selling oil in spot markets was a way to achieve higher prices and even though OPEC members agreed in June 1979 to limit spot sales, high spot prices often proved to be too tempting. While Saudi Arabia, Venezuela, and Algeria refused to participate in the spot market, Iraq, Libya, and Nigeria used it frequently. For a while, Iran even used it exclusively.[29] OPEC members often cited high market prices as a reason to increase their official prices. Ecuador was the first producer to link their long-term contracts to spot prices.[30] Non-OPEC Peru did the same. The market took the lead, and OPEC followed.

With producers turning to the spot market, traders finally gained access to crude oil. While it lasted, the oligopoly of the oil majors gave traders hardly any access to the international crude oil supplies. Traders were mainly involved in dealing in petroleum products, particularly around large petroleum hubs such as Rotterdam. The US was an exception, as a number of very small oil trading companies sprang up as a way of circumventing the government-imposed price controls: '... *in which financiers in the oil market made phony trades in order to evade the spirit (and sometimes the letter!) of the price control rules*'.[31]

Some of those traders, such as the infamous Mark Rich, grabbed the opportunity and allegedly built an empire trading sanctioned Iranian oil.[32] While OPEC was officially hostile to the spot markets, some OPEC members such as Iran effectively facilitated its creation. In a remarkably short time, the share of spot trades rocketed, from just a few per cent, prior to January 1979,[33] to about a quarter, by November of the very same year.

The OPEC members opened up the taps to cash in at these historically high prices. But the party was not to last long. The Iranian production started recovering, just as the demand started to fall. Early in 1980, the market begun to calm down and some cargoes even became 'distressed', struggling to find buyers and trading below official prices.[34]

Between 1979 and 1985, world demand fell by a whopping 8.7 mbd. During the same period, non-OPEC production, including the new North Sea oil,[35] increased by over 5 mbd, resulting in the call on the cartel output of just 14 mbd. Most of the production decline came from Saudi Arabia which was forced to cut by 6.5 mbd in just four years. In 1985, the kingdom was producing only about 3.5 mbd.[36]

To support prices in an environment of falling demand, OPEC had to cut production. In March 1983, at the conference in Vienna, they agreed on a ceiling ('total allowable production') of 17.5 mbd. They also, agreed on maximum production quotas, allocated for each individual country.[37] For the first time ever, OPEC was trying to function as an efficient cartel.

High-quality, sweet, North Sea oil directly competed in Europe with the Nigerian grades of oil, and when in February 1983 the British National Oil Corporation (BNOC) dropped its selling price by $3 a barrel, Nigeria responded by an even greater cut of $5.5 a barrel.[38] In a weak and falling market environment, the official OPEC prices were lagging behind the spot market. At the same time, Britain, Norway, Mexico, USSR, and other producers outside the cartel would sell their oil at prices at which the markets would clear, effectively setting the 'free' spot market price.

Unable to control the global oil exports, OPEC could not defend the prices they fixed. They were also rapidly losing their market share. In response, OPEC agreed to a substantial cut of $5 in price, with Saudi Arabia taking a role of 'swing producer', unilaterally trying to balance the market. Soon, it became obvious that the situation in which the low-cost producers were cutting output, only for the high-cost producers to reap the benefits of those cuts was unsustainable.

In the summer of 1985, the Saudis adopted a simple, but effective strategy to regain their market share. They offered their oil at prices based on the prices of refined, petroleum product, so-called 'netback' prices. The 'netback' price guaranteed refineries profit for every barrel they processed. It was hard to refuse such a deal and the buyers queued up. Oil prices fell below $15 a barrel.

In August 1986 in Geneva, OPEC agreed to substantially cut output to 17 mbd. Spot prices started recovering. At the same time, the Saudi King Fahd insisted that OPEC also defend the official price of $18 a barrel.[39] The cut was not sufficient enough to support this goal, and soon the spot market started trading below this level. The Aramco partners (Exxon, Mobil, Texaco, and Chevron) refused to lift any more Saudi oil unless they were given lower, market-related prices.[40]

So, we come back to the Aramco deal with its partners, mentioned in the introduction of this chapter. The oil trade shifted to benchmark-related, market prices. Premiums and discounts to Brent, WTI, and Dubai were then applied for different types of crude, based on their quality. Soon, the rest of OPEC would adopt this pricing method, and the international trade entered the age of oil benchmarks.

With the US imposing an oil export ban in 1973, WTI could no longer be an international crude oil or serve as a reference for international trade. Asian traders were reluctant to play the role of a price-maker, and Dubai crude continued to trade as a differential to Brent.[41] It was Brent that would carry the mantle of the key global oil benchmark. The rest of the book is dedicated to this most important price of oil.

NOTES

1. See Chalabi (2010, pp. 212–213).
2. Parra (2004, p. 289).
3. Initially, Alaska North Slope (ANS) crude was used as a US benchmark.
4. The invention of the name 'Seven Sisters' is attributed to the head of the Italian state oil company (Eni), Enrico Mattei. They were: 'The five American companies, Standard Oil Company (New Jersey), which became Exxon in 1972; Socony-Vacuum Oil Company, which became

Socony Mobil in 1955 and Mobil in 1966; Standard Oil Company of California, later Chevron; the Texas Company, which became Texaco in 1959; and Gulf Oil Company. Chevron bought Gulf in 1984, and in 1998 Exxon and Mobil merged to form ExxonMobil. The two European companies were Anglo-Persian Oil Company, which changed its name to Anglo-Iranian in 1935 and to British Petroleum in 1954, and the Royal Dutch/Shell group'. https://www.americanforeignrelations.com/O-W/Oil-The-seven-sisters.html#ixzz7hs2Q7zNq.

5. Probably the most readable and entertaining details of the story are in A. Sampson (1988).
6. The agreement stipulated that only the signatories of the agreement could explore and produce oil within the agreed 'red line' encompassing most of the Middle East.
7. http://tatweerpetroleum.com/bahrain-oil-field/#:~:text=In%201923%2C%2051%20year%20old,exchange%20for%20drilling%20water%20wells.
8. US Select Committee (1952, p. 73).
9. For a personal account of the discovery, see Al-Naimi (2016, pp. 16–22).
10. For an excellent study of price discrimination by major oil companies in the Middle East see Leeman (1962, pp. 19–30). For a simple description of the rules to control production, see Sampson (1988, p. 145).
11. Miller (2018, p. 361).
12. Select Committee (1952, p. 356).
13. P. H. Frankel (1969, p. 114).
14. According to a Congressional hearing, it cost about 40 cents (including a 21 cent royalty) to produce oil in Saudi Arabia and only 25 cents (including 15 cents royalty) in Bahrain, compared to the $1.05 price charged to the US Navy. Select Committee (1952, p. 356).
15. Select Committee (1952, pp. 23–29).
16. Adelman (1995, p. 55).
17. Parra (2004, p. 75).
18. A. Sampson (1988, p. 157). In Saudi Arabia, Getty made a $9.5 m down payment and offered higher royalties for exploration and production in the Neutral Zone, between S. Arabia and Kuwait. Getty was later bought by Texaco, which in turn, was 'merged' with Chevron.
    'J. Paul Getty became a billionaire after negotiating a series of oil leases with Saudi Arabia and Kuwait starting in 1949. He soon was being widely reported as the richest man alive'. Where the Getty family fortune came from, CNNMoney, April 1, 2015.
19. D. Yergin (1991, p. 531).
20. Often referred to as: 'Gentlemen's Agreement of Maadi', after the meeting at the informal meeting at the Maadi Yachting Club, Cairo. See Rubino (2008, p. 174). Parra refers to it as 'Mehdi Pact', See Parra (2004, p. 94). Most signatories had no authority to commit to the agreement, so a

clause was inserted to emphasise that the signatories were agreeing in their personal capacities only.

21. https://energyhistory.yale.edu/library-item/opec-treaty-september-14-1960.
22. Garavini (2019, p. 95).
23. Parra (2004, p. 111).
24. OPEC (1968, p. 1184).
25. '*Most precise of all was Sir Eric Drake, the chairman of BP, who called the companies a "tax collecting agency," for both producing and consuming country governments*'. In Adelman (1973, p. 79).
26. See Garavini (2019, p. 203).
27. The value of oil imports to the US alone increased from $8.5 to $25.2 billion, in only one year, from 1973 to 1974. For the other major importers, it increased from $21.1 to $74.8 in the same period.
28. In February 1979, the following countries did it unilaterally: Kuwait, Abu Dhabi, Qatar, and Libya.
29. See Parra (2004, p. 231).
30. See S. Roberts (1984, p. 19).
31. Murphy (2018, p. 2). Also, see D. Amman (2009, p. 117).
32. Copetas (1985, p. 115).
33. New York Times, November 19, 1979.
34. Comptroller General of the United States (1980, p. 10).
35. Between 1982 and 1983, UK production increased from 2.1 to 2.3 mbd and Norwegian production from 0.5 to 0.6 mbd. CIA (1986, p. 1).
36. EIA data. In 1979, total demand was 62.67 mbd and in 1985 it was 53.97 mbd.
37. See https://www.nytimes.com/1983/03/15/business/communique-by-opec.html.
38. https://www.upi.com/Archives/1983/04/08/The-Royal-Dutch-Shell-Group-and-Exxon-Corp-Friday-accepted/5353418626000/.
39. Events are well described in Chalabi (2010, pp. 212–213).
40. Parra (2004, p. 289).
41. See Imsirovic (2014).

REFERENCES

Adelman, M.A. (1973): 'Is the Oil Shortage Real? Oil Companies as OPEC Tax-Collectors', Foreign Policy, No. 9 (Winter, 1972–1973), pp. 69–107.

Adelman, M.A. (1995): 'The Genie Out of the Bottle, World Oil Since 1970', The MIT Press.

Al-Naimi, A. (2016): 'Out of the Desert: My Journey from Nomadic Bedouin to the Heart of Global Oil', Penguin.

Amman, D. (2009): 'The King of Oil', St. Martin's Griffin, New York.

Chalabi, F.J. (2010): 'Oil Policies, Oil Myths', I.B. Tauris & Co. Ltd. London.

CIA, International Energy Statistical Review, various years.

CIA Intelligence Assessment. (1986): The Libyan Oil Industry: Dependence on Foreign Companies, Directorate of Intelligence, January 1986.

Comptroller General of the United States. (1980): 'Report to the Congress of the United States: The United States Exerts Limited Influence on The International Crude Oil Spot Market', August 21, 1980.

Copetas, A.C. (1985): 'Metal Men', Futura Publications.

Frankel, P.H. (1969): 'Essentials of Petroleum, A Key to Oil Economics', Chapel River Press, Andover, Hants.

Garavini, G. (2019): 'The Rise and Fall of OPEC in the Twentieth Century', Oxford University Press.

Imsirovic, A. (2014): 'Oil Markets in Transition and the Dubai Crude Oil Benchmark', Oxford Energy Comment, October 2014.

Leeman, W.A. (1962): 'The Price of Middle East Oil: An Essay in Political Economy', Cornell University Press.

Miller, N.Y. (2018): 'The United States, Britain and the Marshall Plan: Oil and Finance in the Early Post-War Era', Economia e Sociedade, Campinas, Unicamp. IE, https://doi.org/10.1590/1982-3533.2017v27n1art12.

Murphy, R. (2018): 'The Crazy Crude Oil Price Controls of the 1970s', Institute for Energy Research Commentary, April 18.

New York Times, November 19, 1979: 'Spot Oil Market Expanding' by John Geddes, https://www.nytimes.com/1979/11/19/archives/spot-oil-market-expanding-officials-fear-trend-toward-volatile.html.

OPEC. (1968): 'Guidelines for Petroleum Policy in Member Countries', International Legal Materials, Vol. 7, No. 5 (September), pp. 1183–1186, Cambridge University Press.

Parra, F. (2004): Oil Politics, A Modern History of Petroleum, I.B. Taurus Co. Ltd.

Roberts, S. (1984): 'Who Makes the Oil Price? An Analysis of Oil Price Movements 1978–1982', Oxford Institute for Energy Studies WPM, 1984.

Rubino, A. (2008): Queen of the Oil Club, Beacon Press, Boston.

Sampson, A. (1988 ed.): 'The Seven Sisters', Cornet Books.

Select Committee on Small Business, US Senate (August 22, 1952): 'The International Petroleum Cartel, Staff Report to the Federal Trade Commission submitted to the Subcommittee on Monopoly of the Select Committee on Small Business', US Senate, Government Printing Office, Washington.

Yergin, D. (1991): 'The Prize', Simon & Schuster, NY.

CHAPTER 3

Spinning—Like a Circle in a Spiral

Liz Bossley and Nigel Harris

Abstract Following the early discoveries of oil and gas in the UK sector of the North Sea, the Labour government of Harold Wilson enacted The Petroleum and Submarine Pipeline Act which established the British National Oil Corporation ("BNOC"), the British state oil champion. it was also recognised that the market could be a perfect tool for minimising taxation for the larger players in the North Sea oil industry. So-called "tax spinning" is explained in detail in this chapter.

Keywords Government · Taxation · BNOC · Tax spinning

L. Bossley (✉)
Consilience Energy Advisory Group Limited, London, UK
e-mail: lizbossley@ceag.org

N. Harris
Glasgow University, Glasgow, UK

© The Author(s), under exclusive license to Springer Nature
Switzerland AG 2023
A. Imsirovic (ed.), *Brent Crude Oil*,
https://doi.org/10.1007/978-3-031-28232-4_3

27

The phenomenon that oil traders call Brent today (2023) is not what we called Brent when North Sea oil started trading in the late 1970s and 1980s. Today's Brent, in my opinion, is no longer Brent at all, but is an artificially constructed price index, albeit a very useful one.[1] But, this chapter confines itself to discussing the early days of the Brent market and the activity referred to as "spinning".

The evolution of Brent from the prolific physical field in the North Sea discovered in 1971 to the complex suite of contracts and derivatives—physical, forwards, futures, swaps and options and, most importantly, "spreads"—that exist now is a story full of politics and vested interests. It is still evolving.

Genesis

The story of Brent begins with the discovery of gas and then oil in the United Kingdom Continental Shelf ("UKCS"). The Continental Shelf Act of 1964 laid down the rules for the exploration and exploitation of the continental shelf, dividing the UK sector of the North Sea into areas called blocks. Companies were invited to bid for the right to explore for, and produce oil from, these blocks. These bidding opportunities were organised into a series of offshore licencing rounds. To date there have been 33 licencing rounds, the latest of which was in October 2022.

The first UK North Sea oil to come ashore was the Argyll field developed by the American company, Hamilton. That was in 1975 and it was followed closely by production from BP's Forties field just off Aberdeen. The Brent field, which is the subject of this book, was discovered in 1971 by Shell, partnered by Exxon (now ExxonMobil), east of the Shetland Isles in the far North.[2] First Brent production is recorded in 1976, with the first cargoes being exported via the expanding Sullom Voe oil terminal in 1978. The first ever sale of a Brent cargo is reputed to have been a sale to the German company, URBK Rhein Oel, on the tanker, "Donovania", although this is now difficult to verify.

UKCS oil was first found during the Conservative Edward Heath years (1970–1974), but the scene was set for the exploitation of North Sea oil during the labour government years of Harold Wilson (1974–1976) and James Callaghan (1976–1979.)

The Petroleum and Submarine Pipeline Act ("PSPA") of 1975 established the British National Oil Corporation ("BNOC"), the UK state oil company. Lord Frank Kearton, the chairman of Courtaulds, was the first chairman and Chief Executive of BNOC, assisted by the leftward-leaning Sir Alastair Morton and Ian Clark, the Shetland Island Council CEO who had negotiated the Sullom Voe deal with the oil companies.

The corporation was formed in 1975 by taking over the oil assets of the National Coal Board, giving the state oil company access to its own equity[3] barrels for which it had not had to compete in a licencing round with the other oil companies. Additionally, in 1976 BNOC took over a portion of the equity assets of Burmah Oil.

The majority of BNOC's barrels came from government royalty, a tax, which it could elect to take in cash or in kind ("RIC and RIK"), and so-called participation barrels. One of the terms of a licence to explore in the UKCS was the acceptance of a Participation Agreement. This gave BNOC the right to elect on an annual basis to buy 51% of oil produced in the UKCS at a negotiated "market" price, making BNOC one of the biggest oil traders in the North Sea. The BNOC price became the revenue authority's tax reference price.

The objective was to ensure that, if there was ever a repeat of an event like the 1973 Arab oil embargo against states that had assisted Israel during the Yom Kippur war, BNOC would have access to barrels on a strategic basis to protect national interests. Many commercial exploration companies regarded this as nationalisation by another name and there was much resentment of BNOC, who were none too gentle in their negotiation of participation terms.

The terms of the Participation Agreements required BNOC to negotiate a fixed and flat[4] quarterly price at which it would buy Participation Oil and on which RIC and Petroleum Revenue Tax ("PRT") was levied. So the forward oil price curve,[5] if such a concept had then existed, would have been a horizontal line stretching up to 3 months into the future. Mid-quarter revisions were only permitted if there was a "substantial and unforeseen change" in the price of oil after the quarterly price had been set. This reflects the comparatively low daily volatility level that existed in the late 1970s and early 1980s compared with today, with some notable exceptions, such as the Iran–Iraq war.

BNOC was not an oil refiner and only had access to as much storage as its agreements to lift oil from the exporting terminals permitted not only to it, but to the other companies who shared access to the terminal facilities.[6] This was extremely limited. Before the oil producers could sign any oil transportation or lifting agreement with any export terminal or facilities, those agreements had to satisfy BNOC that its ability to take its equity, RIK and Participation barrels was protected. BNOC was a signatory of such agreements.

With nowhere to refine or store oil, BNOC had to sell Participation oil and RIK back to the industry on as close to identical, or back-to-back, terms as it could manage. The quarterly price negotiations between BNOC and the industry were tortuous with the BNOC traders entering into discussions about the price for the forthcoming quarter before the end of each previous quarter with both participation sellers and commercial buyers simultaneously.

In the late 1970s, the spot market was estimated to be about 10% of international daily oil production, compared to today when cargoes are traded many times over in one-off transactions. In the early days BNOC had no authority to sell spot, so all the sales were made into term contracts, typically of one year's duration. Nor had BNOC permission to sell at anything other than its own quarterly price. It was a delicate balancing act to pitch the price as high as possible to maximise the government's tax take, without leaving BNOC with unsold barrels on its hands. Before final agreement of each quarterly price was reached, BNOC had to seek approval of the price from the UK Treasury.

If the producing sellers did not agree with the quarterly price BNOC proposed, they had a right under the Participation Agreement to take the matter to a mutually appointed independent expert for resolution or to arbitration. Buyers who did not like the price had the same right but challenging the BNOC price was a risky strategy because there was a chance that BNOC would not renew the sales contract to the commercial buyer when the time came.

Exodus

The election of a Conservative government in 1979 spelled the beginning of the end for BNOC. The Oil and Gas Enterprise Act of 1982 transferred its equity assets to Britoil, a company subsequently bought by BP in 1988.

During the early years (1980–1985) of the Conservative government (1979–1997), it became increasingly difficult for BNOC to gain approval from Treasury to impose a market-clearing quarterly price on the industry. The price was regularly pitched too high, arguably in response to lobbying from OPEC member states, which certainly took place. In my opinion as a BNOC trader at the time, this strategy played into the hands of a British government bent on the privatisation of the oil sector.

While BNOC was obliged to pay for Participation oil at that inflated rate, it could not sell all its crude back to market participants at the same rate. A progressively larger proportion of BNOC's sales had to be made into the growing spot market, causing that market in one-off, cargo-by-cargo deals to increase its volume and transparency. This was often at prices below the quarterly BNOC prices pushed too high by Treasury edict, either as a doomed attempt to increase tax revenue, or more likely in pursuit of the Thatcher government's privatisation agenda.

As the spot market grew and was widely reported by Price Reporting Agencies ("PRAs") such as Argus, London Oil Report ("LOR") and Platts, traders became more comfortable with abandoning fixed and flat pricing in favour of formula prices. Where before the price of a cargo might be agreed to be $30/bbl, in 1983/4 it became more popular to agree a price formula such as the average of Argus, LOR and Platts spot prices published over a 3–5-day period usually on or around the time of loading of the cargo in question.

This development was not solely in response to the burgeoning volume of BNOC spot sales: increasing market price volatility discouraged many companies from locking themselves into a fixed price for a calendar quarter at a time, or even for a single cargo that may not load for some weeks after the deal date.

Nevertheless, there remained an appetite for fixed and flat price deals entered into for risk management purposes and speculative purposes. Companies who wanted some price certainty and those who simply wanted to punt were happy to buy cargoes for delivery several months forward at a fixed and flat price.

But if a refiner wanted a cargo of the less frequently traded grades of North Sea oil, say Beryl or Flotta or Argyll or Buchan oil, it was unable to buy those grades until the monthly programme of cargoes to be delivered in a given month, M, was issued by the terminal operator, then typically around the middle of month, M-1.[7] For many of the UKCS grades of oil there were only a limited number of cargoes produced each month, so traders were not prepared to go short of those grades, i.e. sell forward without first having purchased.

Buyers, who were unable to buy the less accessible grades of oil several months in advance, were prepared to buy something similar at a fixed and flat price in the forward market with a view to selling that forward grade when it became possible to buy the specific grades of oil that suited their own refineries. There was always plenty of Brent, Ninian and Forties produced, so sellers were prepared to go short of those grades with a view to buying to cover those shorts when the lifting schedules were issued for delivery month M in the middle of the month prior to the month of loading, M-1.

The forward fixed and flat contract initially committed the seller to deliver either Brent, Ninian[8] or Forties ("BNF") to the buyer on giving 15 days' notice of the specific grade and cargo dates that would be delivered. 15 days was chosen because the terminal lifting schedules were issued by mid-month prior to the month of loading, M-1 and so the owner of the cargoes loading in the first few days of the month M were unable to give more than 15 days' notice. Some buyers, particularly refiners who intended to process the cargoes in their own facilities, were uncomfortable with the grade optionality contained in the 15-Day BNF contract. So very quickly 15-Day BNF became 15-Day Brent, the grade of oil which at that time had the highest level of production.

BNOC was quick to avail itself of the 15-Day Brent market, turning a blind eye to its usefulness to the tax minimisation strategies that were to emerge later, and which are discussed below. Although it had no speculative or hedging authority, BNOC had a very large quantity of oil to move each month. So, getting its Brent cargoes placed early into the hands of refiners and traders, of whom there was a rapidly expanding population, made life somewhat easier for the BNOC traders.

The spot cargoes sold by BNOC were at true market prices, in other words often below the treasury-inflated BNOC quarterly term price. BNOC started to haemorrhage money and was dubbed yet another loss-making state enterprise by the Thatcher government, despite the fact that the losses were a direct result of Treasury intransigence. The PSPA was repealed in 1985, abolishing BNOC, and bringing to a close those difficult quarterly price "negotiations". This also served to remove BNOC as the easy target to which OPEC member countries could point when attempting to garner support for high oil prices from the UK government.

Henceforth the tax reference price at which companies paid Royalty, now totally paid in cash, and Petroleum Revenue Tax ("PRT") was no longer the BNOC quarterly price. Now it was placed in the hands of the Oil Taxation Office ("OTO").[9]

REVELATIONS

Petroleum Revenue Tax ("PRT"), a tax on the profits from oil and gas production, was introduced by the Oil Taxation Act ("OTA") of 1975.[10] It was levied on a ring-fenced, field-by-field basis on the sales revenue from the field in question at the end of each six-month chargeable period ending on 30th June or 31st December.

Today the UK North Sea tax regime relies on corporation tax (30%) and a supplementary charge (10%) totalling marginal rates of 40% of the producer's sales price, if it is "arm's length",[11] and at a formula price if it is not. Before 2016, fields that were subject to PRT, paid at a peak rate of 75% after cost recovery deductions, reducing to 50% in 1993. Royalty was initially levied at 12.5% based on wellhead production, but this was gradually phased out between 1983 and 2002.

Before BNOC was abolished by the repeal of the PSPA in March 1985, the tax bill was calculated by reference to the rate of production and sales multiplied by the BNOC quarterly price, less the allowable costs for that field accrued inside the ring fence.[12]

While BNOC's involvement in 15-Day Brent encouraged its growth, it was soon recognised to be the perfect tool for tax minimisation for the oil industry by influencing the tax reference price on which these weighty tax rates were levied, as explained below.

Although PRT was effectively abolished for oil fields that were approved after 16th March 1993 and PRT was permanently reduced to a rate of nil from 1 January 2016, PRT was the compost that fed the growth of the Brent forward market and set in motion a chain of events that led to the proliferation of Brent deals and the development of the "Brent" market as we know it today.

After BNOC was abolished, the tax reference price became the price realised by the producer in "arm's length sales". In other words, if the producer sold its oil to a non-affiliated third party in a deal that was not part of a swap and there was no other consideration than price, this was considered to be arm's length and tax would be levied on the price that the producer actually received.

If the deal at which the producer sold its oil was non-arm's length, such as a sale to its own refiner or as part of a swap, the tax reference price, or Statutory Market Value ("SMV"), using the terminology of the legislation, was a formula price based on PRA published prices.

Before 2006, the SMV for any given month, M, was calculated using a 45-day historic average of published prices from, 1st M-1 to 15th M. This provided a "lookback option" whereby, if prevailing prices around the sales dates for cargoes loading in delivery month M were higher than the cumulative average SMV, then an affiliated company could be inserted between the equity producing company and the ultimate independent buyer. This would make the deal a non-arm's length one. The producer would then pay PRT at an SMV that was visibly lower than the prevailing market price.

After 2006, the system changed. Now, if the oil in question was one of the OTO's reference grades, (dubbed "Category 1 grades": Brent; Forties; Ekofisk; Statfjord; and, Flotta) then the SMV used the published prices averaged over the 2 business days before the notional delivery date ("NDD"), the NDD itself and the two days after the NDD. This has come to be known as "2-1-2" pricing. In the case of non-Brent Category 1 grades the average was adjusted by a grade differential derived from published data averaged over a period commencing 21 days before the NDD and ending 14 days before the NDD. For Category 2 grades, i.e. all the other grades, the quality differential was derived from the rolling average of all arm's length cargoes sold and reported in the 6-month period up to and including the month of lifting.

For the producers of Brent oil that had access to the 15-day market, the opportunity to optimise the tax position was easy:

- Assume the price of 15-Day Brent for delivery, say, six months forward in the month of July was $30/bbl. Any Brent producer that expected to lift[13] a Brent cargo six months forward could in January sell a cargo for delivery in July using the 15-Day Brent market. Once the lifting schedule for July was issued in June, the producer could elect to supply its own equity cargo to satisfy the July sales commitment. It could report this to the OTO and be taxed at an arm's length tax reference price of $30/bbl.
- Alternatively, let's say that a month later, say in February, the price of 15-Day Brent for delivery in July fell to $25/bbl, after the producer had sold a cargo for delivery in July at $30/bbl. The producer who had previously sold at $30/bbl could now buy back that cargo making a profit of $5/bbl on which it would pay only corporation tax of 30% outside the field ring fence. It would simultaneously sell another $25/bbl 15-Day Brent cargo and leave the option open to

report that sale to the OTO/and be taxed at a rate of 75–82.5% on a tax reference price of $25/bbl.

- If the price of oil for July delivery fell further in March to say, $20/bbl, the producer could repeat the whole process and buy back the $25/bbl sale at $20/bbl and sell another 15-Day Brent at $20/bbl to report to the OTO as an equity sale.

This was known as "tax spinning". So long as the price was falling the volume of 15-Day Brent transacted in the market increased. The fact that the producers had initially until the end of the 6-month chargeable period to decide which of their deals they wanted to call arm's length equity, and which were to be non-arm's length equity gave them plenty of time to arrange their sales reporting judiciously to minimise their tax bill.

The OTO got wise to this very quickly and after the price crash of 1986,[14] when prices spiralled down from almost $30/bbl to less than $10/bbl, taking tax revenue with it, a new "nomination scheme" was introduced obliging producers to declare, or nominate, within 2 days of transacting a deal if the contract was to be fulfilled by supplying equity oil or non-equity oil. This was shortened to 1 day in 1993. This seriously curtailed the opportunity to move sales revenue outside the ring fence into a lower tax bracket by shrinking the element of hindsight in the reporting of equity sales to the revenue authorities.

The introduction of the 21-Day Brent Forties Oseberg (BFO) market in 2002 and then the addition of Ekofisk in 2007 made it easier for more producers to spin by bringing more fields into the forward market.

The introduction of the Supplementary Charge ("SC") on production profits in 2002 maintained the incentive to spin revenue outside the ring fence, albeit at a much-reduced tax differential from inside the ring fence.

The heyday of tax spinning was effectively the 1980s, which was exactly the time that the forward Brent market started to trade in 1983 and the International Petroleum Exchange ("IPE"), now the Intercontinental Exchange ("ICE"), launched a successful Brent futures contract in 1988. By the end of the 1980s, Brent had its roots firmly established and went on the become one of the most influential and flexible benchmark grades of oil.

If there remains any doubt about the role of tax in the development of Brent, I will give the last word to Nigel Harris who was one of the premier oil brokers in the Brent market in the 1980s.

BRENT SPINNING—A BROKER'S
PERSPECTIVE—NIGEL HARRIS

Love 'em or hate 'em, brokers were a major contributor to the liquidity of the 15-Day Brent market in the 1980s and remain so today for the markets that have subsequently evolved.

A number of oil companies and trading houses, particularly the management rather than the traders themselves, resented having to pay for the services of a broker. But, as the size of the Brent market mushroomed, the increased coverage provided by brokers, compared to what could be achieved by the traders themselves, proved an essential lubricant to the market.

In the end, the brokers' fees were a small price to pay by traders wanting to achieve the best price. It was as well, of course, a remunerative operation for the brokers, as can be judged from their proliferation, with at least the following 10 actives in the market at the time; Amerex; Aspen; Fearnoil; First National; Fretoil; Nordico; Petroder; Spectron; PVM; and, United.

Spinning was a term to describe the process where Brent equity producers were prepared to buy and sell at the same time, and at the same price. An equity producer in this context, was an oil company that produced oil, specifically Brent System crude oil, in the North Sea. The brokers thought that this might have been something to do with the producers attempting to optimise their fiscal situation, but it's fair to say that none of the brokers around at the time had any intimate knowledge of how the PRT system worked. It is equally fair to say that some knew a bit more than others.

The concept of simply introducing a third party between a buyer and seller had its origins in the use of "Japanese laundries", a not very flattering, but widely used colloquial term, describing the willingness for some Japanese trading houses to go "in between" on a deal, buying from X and selling to Y rather than X selling directly to Y.

Sometimes this was the result of the buyer and seller being unable to deal with each other direct because of differing financial requirements and on other occasions purely driven by these trading houses wanting to increase their turnover on which the traders' bonuses were reported to be calculated. Not all of these trades generated an additional commission, particularly those when the third party was required to make the deal work, but many did. So brokers were already familiar with the concept of introducing a "tweener", another colloquial term, and the processes involved in so doing, when another similar opportunity in the shape of Brent spinning arose.

There was a simplistic understanding that, if a major Brent producer had 10 cargoes to sell in a month, it would make sense to sell 30 cargoes and buy 20 and then declare the 10 lowest priced sales for PRT purposes, if the system so allowed. The more the price changed, and particularly the lower it went, the greater the incentive and maybe they could sell 40 cargoes and buy 30.

Note that Brent was the only grade where this was a realistic option as it was the only grade at that time that had a fully functioning "commodity style" forward market. At this time, in the mid-80s, the 15-Day Brent market was highly liquid and remember that deals for, say, August delivery of Brent could be concluded over a period of many months, probably from April to July (or even mid-August) so that this number of deals was perfectly feasible.

Initially the brokers attempted to put the Brent equity producers in between deals in much the same way that they had with the Japanese trading houses described above. So, for instance, instead of Gatoil selling to Scan Trading, the broker would set the deal as Gatoil selling to an equity producer and then the equity producer selling to Scan Trading at the same price. Although the chance of double commission for the broker was a large incentive, putting another company in between was not without its complications. In the dog-eat-dog world of the brokers, it was, for instance, quite possible that, while the broker was trying to set up the deal described above, another broker might conclude the Gatoil/Scan deal directly leaving the original broker with no deals and zero, rather than double, commission. Also, some traders saw this as their doing a favour for other market participants, not something that was very often offered, if there was nothing in it for them.

An easier way to achieve what the equity producers wanted was for the brokers to set up a "circular deal". When there were 3 companies all looking to both buy and sell and, critically, were prepared to do so at the same price, it became clear that there could be 3 deals done simultaneously as follows:

Equity Producer A to Equity Producer B $22.50/barrel
Equity Producer B to Equity Producer C $22.50/barrel
Equity Producer C to Equity Producer A $22.50/barrel

All company A needed to know was that they were buying from company C and selling to Company B. There was no need for the broker to advise that B was selling to C at the same time, so the counterparties did not know that they were part of a circle. The price was always set in line with market conditions at the time. As the price moved, and particularly as it fell, another circular deal could be set up and in extreme occasions this could sometimes be just an hour or so later, with the direction of the circle reversed.

> Equity Producer A to Equity Producer C $22.00/barrel
> Equity Producer C to Equity Producer B $22.00/barrel
> Equity Producer B to Equity Producer A $22.00/barrel

This process also resulted in clear possibilities for "book outs".[15] So, the producers could not only achieve a degree of fiscal efficiency, but a lot of the potential Brent chain credit exposure and operational problems could be mitigated. Again, each individual producer only needed to be told whom they were selling to and buying from, with no need for any advice about the third deal in the circle.

In the case described above the broker will have earned 6 commissions for minimal effort. Happy days! At this time in the mid-80s a typical commission was 1c/barrel, and a Brent cargo was 500,000 barrels, so $30,000 commission was very nice. If the price continued to fall the whole operation could be repeated, perhaps introducing equity producer D and equity producer E into the process.

On some occasions equity producer, A might say, for instance, that they would prefer not to sell to equity producer B today or that they would like to buy from equity producer E, if conditions permitted. This was quite possibly for book-out considerations and was not uncommon in the market generally, but it helped the broker set the "direction" of the circle accordingly.

At the end of the day, the reasons for the producers pursuing these deals were of no concern to the broker. Indeed, though some of the brokers had some idea of what may have been going on, particularly those with employees who had previously worked in major oil companies, they did not consider it to be their role to ask questions, but just worked to cover their clients' requirements.

These good times for the brokers didn't last long. Commission levels generally fell and increasingly the equity producers became less willing to do these deals. Some would now either want a 1c margin to do this type of business or would do it, but not pay a commission. Obviously, the former was impossible unless one of the other parties was prepared to take a 1c hit, though on very rare occasions that might happen. But if 2 of the 3 players were prepared to pay commission it still made sense for the broker to put the deal together. Even if only one of the participants paid commission, it still made sense for the broker. But with commissions reduced to $0.5 per barrel and only one payer in each circular deal, the commission from the process above would now be $5000 rather than $30,000, and so not such happy days!

The interest in spinning from the equity holders faded through the 80s, most likely a result of changes in tax procedures, and the easy money, some would say free money, for brokers faded with it.

The role of brokers would, of course, remain, but would now be back not only in the traditional Brent market, finding a buyer and seller that were prepared to deal at the same price, but increasingly in the shape of various Brent-derived swaps that developed.

NOTES

1. "It's Brent, Jim, but not as we know it." https://ceag.org/liz-out-loud/
2. Oil historians may recall that the negotiations between the Shetland Island Council and the oil majors about the building of Sullom Voe was parodied in the much-romanticised Bill Forsyth 1983 movie, "Local Hero". This concerned the thwarted attempts by a fictitious oil company to acquire land to build an oil refinery on a Scottish east coast beauty spot. The difficult "local hero" was said to be based on Ian Clark, the Shetland Island county clerk and a CEO.
3. Equity barrels are oil produced from a field in which a company has effective ownership by virtue of its licence agreement. Equity production is then subjected to royalty, participation and other taxes.
4. A price expressed at the time the deal is transacted as $X/bbl. The price is therefore known at the outset, and does not emerge at a later date from a price formula in the contract.
5. The forward oil price is a graphic representation of the prices at a single point in time at which buyers and sellers will trade the same oil for delivery in different future time periods.

6. Excluding fuel storage depots managed by the Oil and Pipeline Agency on behalf of the Ministry of Defence. Although the OPA was established by the PSPA, BNOC never had access to these depots.
7. This now happens during the second half of M-2.
8. Brent and Ninian were delivered through separate pipelines to S. Voe and traded as separate grades of oil until August 1990 when they were commingled to become Brent Blend.
9. This is now in the hands of the Office for Budget Responsibility.
10. The OTA was amended by the Petroleum Revenue Tax Act of 1980. The effect of the latter was to accelerate the payment of PRT at a time when the new Thatcher government, elected in 1979, was strapped for cash.
11. A deal considered to be arm's length if the buyer and seller are two companies that are not affiliated in any way and there is no consideration between the two parties other than price.
12. A ring fence is an accounting device designed to isolate the profit calculation for a given oil field from costs and revenue accrued by the field owner in relation to any other field or affiliated company. This prevents companies importing costs from low tax-paying fields to high tax-paying fields.
13. Lifting means taking a cargo out of shared storage at the terminal facilities in accordance with a lifting schedule issued by the terminal operator in the month prior to the month of delivery.
14. This price crash was attributable to OPEC netback pricing.
15. A book-out is when a string of deals is settled in a cash up and down the chain, rather than by physical delivery. In a book-out only the difference between the deal price and a chosen reference price is transferred between the parties to any link in the chain, rather than the full value of the cargo.

BIBLIOGRAPHY

"25 years of UK North Sea Exploration" J.M (Miles) Bowen, 1991.

BP Statistical Review of World Energy 71st edition, 2022.

"Local Hero" 1983, directed by Bill Forsyth. https://www.cineaste.com/spring 2020/local-hero.

Oil and Gas Enterprise Act of 1982. https://www.legislation.gov.uk/ukpga/1982/23/contents.

Oil Taxation Act of 1975. https://www.legislation.gov.uk/ukpga/1975/22.

Principles of Petroleum: Then and Now", Paul J. Frankel. The Energy Journal 1989.

Revenue Analysis Apportionment and Hedging, Consilience 2022. https://ceag.org/oil-field-hedging-software-more-detail/.

The Continental Shelf Act of 1964. https://www.legislation.gov.uk/ukpga/1964/29/contents.

The Petroleum and Submarine Pipeline Act ("PSPA") of 1975, repealed in 1985. https://www.legislation.gov.uk/ukpga/1975/74/contents.

The UK Government Oil Taxation Manual last updated 22nd December 2021h. https://www.gov.uk/hmrc-internal-manuals/oil-taxation-manual/.

"Trading Crude Oil: the Consilience Guide", 2014. https://ceag.org/shop/trading-crude-oil-books/trading-crude-oil/.

CHAPTER 4

Brent—Creating Exceptionalism

Colin Bryce

Abstract The fiscal regime and liberalisation policies in the 1980s made "… the senior executives of big oil realise that there was a whole new revenue stream to be captured by speculating in oil markets". This chapter covers the development of the whole ecosystem of players in the Brent market in rich detail. It is a wonderful record of how various players, and banks in particular, contributed to the price discovery and risk management using swaps, options and other derivative instruments from the financial markets. Eventually, one such "partials Brent" market led to the development of the first Brent oil exchange, the International Petroleum Exchange or IPE.

Keywords Liberalisation · Speculation · Brent · Banks · IPE

C. Bryce (✉)
Hitchin, United Kingdom
e-mail: bryce@laundrycottagestud.com

A. Imsirovic (ed.), *Brent Crude Oil*,
https://doi.org/10.1007/978-3-031-28232-4_4

THE FIRST SULLOM VOE CARGO

Late in the day on 28 November 1978, the master of the Shell oil tanker, Donovania, received the radio call that he had been waiting for.[1] She had, for some time, been at anchor in the "roads", one of the holding areas close to the coastline of the Shetland Islands.

Ongoing negotiations had been taking place between the owners of the newly constructed, but as yet incomplete, Sullom Voe Terminal and their landlords, the Shetland Islands Council, on the matter of who would pay for costs arising were there to be a pollution incident. This deadlock had delayed the loading of the first cargo of oil that had been delivered through the Brent System pipeline to Sullom Voe.

Agreement on the splitting of costs should a spillage incident take place was finally reached, and the call came to the Donovania to proceed to berth, the first of many occasions she would so do in her career as a cross North Sea oil tanker.

That first cargo had been sold in advance to the German refining company, URBK. Their well known and strident London representative, Doris Balzer,[2] was not someone whose displeasure one wanted to incur, and so news of the commencement of loading was received with sighs of relief at the offices of BNOC, the seller of the oil.

So commenced the remarkable story of "Brent"—the crude oil[3] (named after the Scottish lochs Broom, Rannoch, Etive, Ness and Tarbert) and, more importantly, the brand that would come to dominate the oil trading industry and popular conception of oil trading across the globe for the succeeding forty plus years.

Dated Brent is the benchmark against which up to 70% of the world supply of physical crude oil has been priced. "BFOET" Brent is the traders forward contract of choice and ICE Brent is the single largest futures contract referencing an internationally traded crude oil. This is the story of the process and the identification of the enabling factors that led to the creation of the exceptional and resilient entity—the towering cumulus of fossil fuel trading—that was, and still is, Brent.

THE BUSINESS OF TRADING

Brent oil had already hit the market before November 1978, although this was production which had been delivered from an offshore loading point[4] known as "Brent Spar", but it was only with the commencement of loadings from Sullom Voe that the early buccaneering period of oil trading began to be replaced by a "movement" consisting of companies, people, places and products that would enable the creation of the multi-billion dollar industry of oil trading. It is a business which reaches into everyone's life, from the price of hydrocarbon-derived consumables to how we travel, heat and cool ourselves through to the value of dividends from the largest oil companies that affect the worth of our pensions.

The first oil spot trade was probably the 1969 purchase of Tunisian crude oil by Alan Flacks of the commodity house, Philipp Brothers[5] and it presaged a period of inconvenient geo-political awakening in oil producing countries. Until then, oil had been priced, shipped, refined and distributed by an oligopoly of sorts, whose main players were known as the Seven Sisters.

Following the OPEC policies in 1970s, the "Sisters" lost their hegemony in the oil markets and looked for oil elsewhere. Originally, the "Sisters" believed that any hope of finding significant quantities of oil under the North Sea was most unlikely. That BP had commissioned the construction of a fleet of ULCC'S to be delivered from yards in Japan and Korea which would fuel enhanced economics in the shipment of oil from the Middle East via the Cape (and thus avoiding Suez) suggests that the company indeed viewed the North Sea as marginal (those same ULCC'S would never carry oil and were, in the main, sailed directly from shipyard to locations in Greece and Pakistan to be laid up—two of them by this writers father as a Captain with BP Shipping).[6]

Security of supply became the main concern of governments. While the US were well placed to face down the embargo placed on many countries at the time of the Yom Kippur War in 1973, the UK and Europe were not. And big oil was not about to help, as demonstrated by BP Chairman, Sir Eric Drake's rebuffal of UK Prime Minister Edward Heath, when he insisted that BP must ensure supply to the UK over other countries and customers.

Not 3 years earlier in 1970, Sir Eric had stated that the hope of finding significant quantities of oil under the North Sea was most unlikely.

Which is all a touch surprising as it was shortly thereafter in 1971, that both the Forties field and the Brent field were discovered in the North Sea. While they were not the first discoveries, they were game changers as they were world class in size. A little earlier, Norway had found Ekofisk, and it became clear that with this geological surprise (at least to Sir Eric) the supply situation for the UK and Europe was improving.

The Trader and the Tax Collector

The British government struggled to get to grips with the bonus under the North Sea. In her unpublished Ph.D. thesis[7] Stephanie Hoopes paints a picture (from extensive interviews of the sadly long passed) of governmental shilly-shallying, interdepartmental rancour and pedantic fumbling within the Civil Service and Ministries, ideological flip flopping and a succession of weak ministers and officials being bullied by aggressive industry veterans.

Harvie points out in "Fools Gold"[8] revealingly that the memoirs of the main political actors of the time—Wilson and Thatcher, pay little attention to the subject of North Sea oil.

In the lengthy lead up to the establishment of The British National Oil Company (BNOC), the perceived objectives for the entity ranged from purely ensuring security of supply to the UK to being solely an advisor to government. Was the real job of BNOC to stabilise prices or perhaps to keep them high to maximise the tax take or perhaps, as was clearly the case with the discovery of gas 10 years earlier, to keep prices low for the consumer?[9] The evidence is unclear, and the objectives remain, in hindsight, contested. The final form, though, left BNOC bearing at least two burdens.

The first of these was the creation of a company with both an agency and a principal role—so-called dual capacity. This, along with BNOC's "notoriously antagonistic approach"[10] to the owners of North Sea oil when charged by their governmental masters to negotiate the state's participation terms, led to a mistrust that deprived the company of having any friends in the market to turn to at times of need. While on its own this element does not seem relevant in the story of Brent, it came to be important as a consequence of the other big burden.

BNOC was legally able to elect to take a far greater volume of crude oil than was needed for refining in the UK should security of supply needs kick in (state "participation").[11] On top of this, there was no provision for the company to be able to refine oil or to store it. Nor was there more than a limited charter to trade. BNOC further had to buy on long-term fixed contracts and sell on short-term deals, in many cases, on the spot market resulting in losses in a falling market. Without friends and with quite hostile undertones coming from the oil companies, even if the company's traders had good relations with counterparts, BNOC had nowhere to turn but to the public purse to relieve supply stress and cover losses. It was finally abolished in 1985.

Yet, from this distress, came, crucially, a surplus of oil which fuelled activities already underway on the embryonic spot physical markets as they developed over the first half of the 1980s.

Yet the BNOC fault line surplus, especially as it arose in 1983–1985, was only one enabler in the process of innovation that created present day oil markets.

A second important reason for the future development of markets was the peculiarity of the UK fiscal regime and its effect on the embryonic Brent complex. An especially eloquent summary of the importance of tax to the market development process appeared in Weekly Petroleum Argus in 1985. Jan Nasmyth, the doyen of energy journalists, is quoted as saying "the Brent market became a mechanism that reconciles the practical exigencies of the oil industry with the requirements of the tax collector and.... the independent trader has been called into being to assist in the process".[12]

The important topic of tax (and of this "process") is dealt with separately in this book but suffice to say for the present purposes, the tax regime which levied one rate or the Petroleum Revenue Tax (PRT) upstream and another lesser rate (Corporation Tax) downstream, played into the hands of the integrated oil companies who, through buying and selling multiple cargoes of oil within a tax period, could determine ex post which ones to declare as equity (and thus PRT) and which as refining and trading cargoes (Corporation Tax). The gains to be made in this game of "spinning" were legion. First mentioned in the industry press (PIW) in April 1981, it grew rapidly in importance both for market volume growth and for integrated company revenues. According, again to Petroleum Argus in April 1985,[13] "for every dollar off the price, an integrated company can save 36 cents per barrel by transferring profit from production" due to the different rates of tax levied on their upstream and downstream activities.

Brent Teething Pains

The fiscal enabler was clearly a necessary condition for the growth of trading, yet it was not sufficient—not by a long way! There is another less well considered argument to be made that it was not the fiscally driven spinning per se that was the main enabler, but rather the discovery in the offices of the senior executives of big oil that there was a whole new revenue stream to be captured by speculating in oil markets (few in business rely simply on tax breaks for a long-term strategy)! They knew when to buy and when to sell as, happily, big oil had much more information about refining margins or shipping patterns or production profiles than did any other participants in these new markets. That was worth protecting. Not only was there a corporate benefit foreseen, but the very individuals engaged in trading clearly believed that there was also a personal upside to promulgating active trading. The independent trade houses flocking to the honeypot were paying big salaries and the oil company "bench traders" were in great demand. Everyone wanted the boom to continue and, indeed, to expand.

By 1984–1985 according to Robert Mabro,[14] there were some 125 participants in the Brent market and by late 1986, this writer had a total list of 155 companies for he and colleagues to cover in his contact list. Of course, the majors were all there, but many were independent traders also. Aside from the big names of Phibro (estimated to be handling 60 cargoes per month by late 1984), Trans World Oil (TWO) and Marc Rich (experts in achieving difficult things in difficult places), there were the traders supported by ultra-high net worth. Bomar were rumoured to be backed by the Rothschild empire, Sirco by Sears Roebuck, Gotco by the Hinduja family and Carey by an ex-mayor of New York. Tradax also arrived as a division of agricultural house, Cargill. The European and US refiners all had London offices and traders and the Japanese Shoshas[15] were active in providing a low-cost credit intermediation service (known colloquially as "sleeving").

How can we deduce that the self-interest motives of the milieu were valid factors in the enablement process? Perhaps the clearest demonstration of the importance of maintaining momentum comes from a consideration of the lengths that the most important incumbents (people and companies) went to in order to protect the market from harm. The self-regulatory actions of Shell in particular,[16] but also of BP and others, saved the markets from collapse on enough occasions to have been considered heroic and at a juncture when the market had fallen into a certain level of disrepute.

The activities of the Brent market were viewed by the industry media with, at best, suspicion—"… a monster… to which no prudent man would willingly entrust oil supply"[17] was the view of Jan Nasmyth in March 1985. In the same month he wrote in his Weekly Petroleum Argus

leader that "North Sea Oil in the eighties has become a gambling counter".[18] With other associated oil products markets being referred to at
the time as "Boston Bingo" and "Russian Roulette", the association with
betting was unfortunate.

The market was under the cosh and the potentially most damaging
instances of market misbehaviour were the frequent attempts by members
of the trading "club" (the incumbent market participants of the time) to
orchestrate market squeezes and to extract excess payment to release those
on the wrong side from their obligations.

In this context, the name of Trans World Oil (owned by John Deuss,
supposedly seen by some in the market as a Bond-like mysterious figure)
appears at the head of most people's lists and the subject is well covered
in detail elsewhere. Separately, instances of fraud and non-performance
possibly formed more of a threat to the continued good standing of the
market in the mid-80s.

Contract abrogation by Gatoil Services in 1985 was the most serious
non-performance issue to hit the Brent market by that stage and a resolution organised by Shell and aided by senior industry figures demonstrated
the degree of desire to keep the show on the road.

A subsequent instance of fraud and unapproved trading at the German
industrial company, Kloeckner, found the principal of Gatoil at work
behind the scenes (he eventually served a prison sentence in Switzerland)
but also found one of the senior industry mediators from the Gatoil event
thrust into the limelight to cleanse the Kloeckner books.[19]

Morgan Stanley's hiring of Nancy Kropp in 1984 proved to be an
inspired move. The smart, gregarious and well-connected Ms. Kropp had
arrived on Wall St from Sun Oil and held all the credentials that would
help her new employers identify themselves as "oil people". Along with
her newly hired colleague, John Shapiro and internal transferee, Marc
Crandall, son of the crusty CEO of American Airlines, Bob Crandall and
Morgan's youngest ever Executive Director (later to be one of the four
founding members of Trafigura), the three executives set the scene for a
business that would eventually generate MS in excess of $3.5 billion in
good years for the bank.

Morgans' almost immediate Wall St follower into the oil trading fray,
the Goldman Sachs owned, J Aron, took a different route and started
out with two senior metals traders, Steve Hendell and Steve Semlitz, who
chose a paper trading entrée to oil markets as opposed to Morgans' more
physical trading approach.

Ms. Kropps' emotionally intelligent approach to business relationships, her reputation as likeable and fair and her extensive book of business contacts marked her out as a key facilitator in the Gatoil resolution arrived at by industry bigwigs.

In 1988, when the Brent market was suffering from overly frequent crises, the Klockner debacle burst into the open. Ms. Kropp was at Gatwick Airport having announced her retirement and was about to fly off to a relaxed new life with her art dealer husband, when a friend contacted her to insist that she made an important call immediately.[20]

The call she was asked to make was to the late Dr. Alfred Herrhausen, the then Chair of Deutsche Bank and he demanded that Ms. Kropp abandon her plans and fly immediately to Frankfurt to help minimise losses in liquidating the portfolio of unapproved transactions. In all probability, it had been her friend in URBK, the feisty Frau Balzer—she had been the buyer of that first Brent cargo back in 1978—that had recommended her up the German financial sector chain.

In due course, the Klockner books were straightened out for a cost well below the anticipated loss (reportedly originally some $450 million reduced to $303 million[21] the latter number cited in the *New York Times* report on the extradition of Gatoil principal, Khalil Ghattas from Switzerland to West Germany). This was due in no small part to Ms. Kropps' assiduous use of her contact book, her careful market presence in the liquidation process and a steel fist that had always been there, but mostly had remained hidden within a velvet glove, throughout her career.

The Brent show was kept on the road, the bench traders' self-interest opportunities for upgrading their financial prospects within the growing industry were preserved and the oil companies trading profit gravy train rolled on. Whew...!

The Wall Street Refiners

Equally crucial in the enablement process at this point was the emergence of the so-called "Wall St Refiners" in the energy space. Coming from backgrounds in Agriculture and Metals price risk management, the Wall Streeters viewed markets in a very different way to the oil trade.

One Aron employee is quoted as saying "we don't buy oil, we buy value".[22] In these short few words, one discovers the guiding principles of the bank's trading activities. It came to be known as relative value trading. They had little interest in trying to guess whether the price of oil might go up or down rather they determined by assiduous research where they believed the equilibrium value of one quality or location, or time horizon of oil should sit in relation to any other. So, if, for example, they believed that the difference between jet fuel and gas oil in Singapore should be $30 per ton but it was trading at only $20 per ton, then they would buy jet and sell gas oil in the hope that the spread would re-equilibrate (or mean revert as the lingo went). The mining of temporal, spatial and quality basis risk would be a profitable avenue for these companies to explore for years to come.

Using this logic, the banks could solicit business from traders and corporate entities experiencing a price risk at the market interface, take on that price risk and hedge it with an alternative dis-equilibrated product elsewhere and await re-equilibration. Do enough of this across a disparate portfolio and one turns the probabilities in one's favour.

Wall Street was bringing a seriousness of purpose to Brent trading and their traders lunched at the desk. The innovative characteristics of their employees are well demonstrated by the way in which one trader who, wanting access to CNN (which did not exist in the UK at the time) during the first Gulf War, purchased a satellite dish in London's Tottenham Court Road, set it up on the roof of his office (held in place by sandbags blagged from a nearby building site) and so managed to receive the CNN service as required!

The novel nature of their contribution to the concept of trading in oil markets cannot be overstated, most especially at a moment when enhanced transparency in markets was inconveniently militating against the privileged knowledge position of big oil. The contribution of the Wall St Refiners to the financialisation of oil markets and their rapid maturation in the second half of the 1980s didn't stop with relative value trading.

By 1986, Marc Crandall and David Solomon respectively at MS and Aron had promulgated a trade in over-the-counter oil options to sit alongside the already existing, but less flexible, cleared options market hosted by the New York Mercantile Exchange. That venue had offered a futures market in the US domestic crude oil, WTI, since 1983 and the futures complex had played its part in enabling the relative value trading activities of the Wall Streeters, who used it extensively to hedge their own positions.

Over in Europe, the International Petroleum Exchange had, without success, tried on successive occasions in 1983 and 1985 to launch a futures contract in Brent Crude oil. With these failures, hedgers in Europe had to either utilise the 15-day Brent market with its fixed cargo size of 500,000 barrels plus or minus 5% or choose to hedge a European risk with a US landlocked domestic crude, West Texas Intermediate (WTI), albeit with a more exact volume match.

And so, in 1988, Wall Street invented "Partial Brent". It was conceived at a Morgan Stanley traders' meeting in late 1987 in a windowless room in 1251 Avenue of the Americas, the firm's global HQ. The business units' European co-heads (this writer and his colleague) were dispatched back home to write a contract and market it to their oil company friends as a more exact hedge for their palette of market risks.

Creating an important new hedging instrument is well remembered as being especially intellectually satisfying and the product was eagerly adopted by a group of enlightened users. Initially, they were Enterprise Oil, Petronor, ICI, LASMO, Elf Aquitaine and Conoco. The appetite for this product grew rapidly and within less than a year, the IPE were able to launch a futures contract for a third time—and this time with success—having been shown the way by Wall Streeters innovation. The enhanced transparency of the futures venue versus the over-the-counter[23] opacity of the Partials market, along with an easier position exit process, led to that market being usurped by futures, but the credit remained with Wall Street (a not dissimilar process would occur 10 years later when MS and GS helped found ICE)-(the electronic exchange).

The next important product development in 1989, came not from Wall Street but from Main Street and specifically from the oil company Mobil. Physical oil—Dated Brent for example—responded to different market influences than did its forward equivalent, 15-day Brent. In their desire to manage their physical risks more precisely, Mobil sent out enquiries to the Wall Street Refiners and others to invite them to take the other side of the "Dated for Paper Contracts for Difference".

This was a reasonably complex swap product to trade and hedge but was one which was to secure significant revenues for providers over many years to come as the temporal behavioural characteristics of the relationship became familiar to some, but not to all participants in the oil markets (the so-called "transition roll"[24] was a profitable trading relationship for some).

Petroleum Intelligence Weekly (PIW), in a Special Report in December 1990 stated that this product "improves the hedge available through trading in the forward Brent market by reducing the basis risk between the physical wet cargo market and forward prices". It did much more than this. One providers marketing literature at the time[25] stated that "Dated / Paper swaps can lock in a margin, assist in transferring a floating price to a fixed price, partially hedge backwardation, alter the timing of one's exposure to market price, allow speculators to go price short on the physical market without the actual physical position and more precisely hedge actual risk".

The major oil companies had become accustomed to hedging their risks and benefited enormously from the liquidity provided to them by Wall St. They could now more fully hedge their foreign physical cargoes that were priced by reference to the published price of Dated Brent. This was Mobil's motivation and became the motivation of others with Dated Brent related physical exposure, such as Shell and Chevron.

One employee of Chevron at the time received an official commendation for his "Contribution to the development and industry standardisation of the Dated to 15 Day spread" in 1989. One can only imagine his pride in receiving such a humbling citation!

At a later stage, this market developed a certain notoriety for the perceived games being played by the most influential players trying to persuade the price reporting agency Platts, that the benchmark should be set at a value advantageous for their trading positions. Yet the market has fought off such pressure (with the muscular assistance of Platts led by their price setter Jorge Montepeque) and it remains the key instrument for price risk management and speculation.

One must, then, count the Wall St Refiners amongst the most influential enablers of the founding period of traded energy markets and their necessary involvement in the innovative process which was so important in the creation of the multibillion-dollar business that now exists is clear to see.

The innovative process did not stop with CFD's. Louise Murray, a go-ahead young Scottish trader with BP popularised the refinery margin hedge, allowing refiners to manage time and manufacturing risk and the Price Fixation deal, which allowed buyers or sellers to close a supply or distribution deal without having to price that deal at the same moment, was an import from agriculture market. As the complexity of traded market instruments increased, so were the "good old boys" replaced by the mathematicians. Numeracy trumped clubability!

PLACE AND PEOPLE

Pulling together all the enabling elements was the crucial influence of "place" in the algorithm.

To employ the language of the geographer, the influence of "place" in the story of the genesis of oil markets was to provide a setting for the creation of "a unique set of social and economic relations"[26]. This is the simple concept of "clustering"—the benefits of closeness and contiguity.

The Rotterdam Spot Market never existed in Rotterdam, nor did a market emerge in say, Dubai (still a desert lightly criss-crossed by a few lines of tarmac when this writer visited in 1984), even despite the huge volumes of oil sourced from these places. The early days of the buccaneers in Madrid and Paris saw no follow through and Norway was on the wrong side of the North Sea Trench.

Arguably, it was the bifurcation of futures trading based in New York and physical oil trading based in Houston that split the possibility of the beneficial effect of the cluster working in favour of the US becoming the centre of oil trading at this juncture.

So, it was the bright lights of London, with its admired UK legal system, Mrs Thatcher's embrace of markets, the Big Bang and the restaurants, bars and other (of interest to some) venues of Mayfair that attracted the crowd. There was a lot more going on there than in, say, Rotterdam or Riyadh. Brent found its market location and expression to be in London.

And this innovative group, characterised in a Texas Monthly article in 1984 as "financial speculators, con artists, impoverished aristocrats, former tennis pro's, ambitious young college and B school grads looking to make their fortune as fast as they can" thrived as a close club of frequent lunchers, Wimbledon, Lords and Twickenham attendees and a few Tokyo Joe's nightclub stragglers. They were the "movement" that made stuff happen. To which one may add the odd dilletante, ex-mercenary and even the ex-goalie of Hibernian FC.[27]

The effect of this cluster on the process should not be underestimated. Without the exchanges of view and information over long lunches, would the concept of "spinning" ever have occurred to the Conoco trading manager credited with its inception?[28] Would the market in cargoes of Brent/Ninian/Forties at Sellers Option have developed as an early standardised tradable instrument and would it have morphed into 15-day Brent if the equity holders, integrated company users and traders been located across the globe as opposed to being cheek by jowl in Central London? It is most unlikely that the necessary creative subtleties could have been formulated by telephone (a large suitcase sized portable object or a clumsy looking Bakelite contraption at that stage) or by telex! The technological limitations of the time are easily overlooked.

Additionally, the presence of Shell and BP, major producers and market players in London, added to the "making of the market. Without them it would not exist".[29]

So, the contiguities of "place" mattered a lot and London mattered a lot. So did people, (those who, in the words of one ex national oil company trading executive),[30] were "lucky enough to work, or rather more accurately, get paid in this industry".

Little of consequence occurs in business or life through the passive acceptance of the status quo and without the innovative spark of the challenger and disrupter.

The oil market and the Brent story were, fortunately, not short of these characters. Once one has eliminated the chancers and the scallywags, the real change agents and innovators emerge. Although other names, perhaps more widely recognisable to a 2020s audience, were later to prove their worth (names such as Jeff Sprecher of ICE, the late Ian Taylor of Vitol being good examples), the names of the enabling days are important to recognise.

There were the early buccaneers such as Alan Franks, Marc Rich and Pincus Green of Phillip Bros. There were the "famously abrasive and fearsome"[31] BNOC CEO Alistair Morton, the Shell trading manager enablers and market "regulators", Peter Lane and Peter Ward and Phibros' Andy Hall, widely considered the finest trader of the era.

Special mention should be made of the contribution of BP to the "movement". That organisations' habit of rotating its best minds through the Supply and Trading department, often on their way to the Board (individuals such as David Simon, Brian Gilvary, Iain Conn and many others),[32] meant that this company had market savvy presence right to the top level and this encouraged them to support, participate in and protect the Brent and allied markets when its careful incubation was required. BP have also been, consistently, the main suppliers of talent to the independent trading industry.

CONCLUSION

This chapter and account of the growth of a movement and a multi-billion-dollar venue for commerce has attempted to understand (albeit in shorthand) the enabling factors and complex process of inception and maturation of the Brent market during a hectic 10-year period roughly according to the 1980s—a period when the brand that is Brent and a new asset class, oil, were created. In particular, the influence of the government created oil surplus in the UK, the self-interest of the individuals involved in the embryonic activity, their clustering in London and their particular character traits are as least as important in the process as the often-enumerated view that the fiscal regime and legal system in the UK and the presence of nearby oil fields were key. They may have been necessary, but they were collectively insufficient.

With the benefit of hindsight and the ex-participants' gaze, a renewed interpretation, challenged and contested though it will surely be, is worth a pause for thought.

In all of this there are perhaps lessons to be gained for the currently somewhat disorganised but hugely expanded US Gulf WTI crude oil export complex, of so much potential in its ability to lead a changing of the guard in oil benchmarking.

And there may well be lessons for the energy transition milieu as firms, individuals and governments attempt to find their individual sweet spot in what may well be the next markets "movement".

NOTES

1. Shetland Times 29/11/1978.
2. Also known as Rhein Oel, this German refiner was represented in London by Helmar Schank and Doris Balzer, the former a quietly spoken, very formal individual and the latter being somewhat more outgoing and strident.
3. Shepherd, Mike (2015): Oil Strike North Sea, Luath Press p. 173.
4. Brent Spar was a standalone oil loading facility located offshore.
5. Ammann, David (2009, p. 5).
6. I recall one vessel arriving near our home at the BP Finnart Oil Terminal in Scotland directly from launch. The vessel was stripped of any items that were not tied down (by locals, friends and family) before setting sail for Piraeus in Greece and permanent lay-up. Unladen, the colossal ULCC dominated even the dramatic fjord landscape of Loch Long and a fleet of bicycles were even kept on board to move up and down the deck.

7. Hoopes, Stephanie M. (1994).
8. Harvie C. (1994, p. 8).
9. Atkinson F. and Hall S. (2016): Oil and the British Economy, p. 19.
10. Hoopes, Stephanie M. (1994, p. 212).
11. Hoopes refers to Ministers and Civil Servants being surprised when BNOC exercised all their Participation rights.
12. See Weekly Petroleum Argus April 1985.
13. Weekly Petroleum Argus (10/04/1983), p. 1.
14. Mabro et al. (1986, p. 202).
15. Sogo Shoshas were Japanese conglomerates with interests across business and trading. The seven active companies were C Itoh, Marubeni, Mitsui, Mitsubishi, Nissho Iwai, Sumitomo and Toya Menka. The performance of their London offices was measured by turnover and they were eager to credit intermediate between companies who could not deal with each other in return for a small fee and for the turnover trading created.
16. Shell would release additional cargoes to a squeezed market to help avert non performance.
17. Weekly Petroleum Argus 08/03/1985.
18. Weekly Petroleum Argus (08/03/1985), p. 1.
19. Kloeckner were a German steel and base metal trader who had become involved in trading oil on the 15 day market as a speculative activity. The principal of Gatoil, Khalil Gattas, had conspired with Kloeckner executive, Wolfgang Zeschmar by persuading him to buy and sell 15-Day Brent for Gatoil, but in Kloeckners name (Gatoil being somewhat unwelcomed as a market counterparty), without his companys' permission. When the trades began to show significant losses, a cover-up operation was mounted which was eventually discovered and Zeschmar was arrested and subsequently jailed.
20. Gilpin K. (1994): Trying to Rescue a Soured Oil Bet *New York Times* 25/09/1994 and personal recollection.
21. *New York Times* (08/09/1989).
22. according to David Hufton, head broker at PVM London at the time.
23. An over the counter market (OTC) is a private market between commercial entities lacking the transparency of a public futures market and also having less onerous financial guarantee conditions (margin),at least in this early period.
24. See Ford, J. (2016); Depression, Oil Trading, pp. 81–84.
25. Internal Morgan Stanley sales literature.
26. Agnew John (1987): The United States in the World Economy–A Regional Geography Cambridge University Press.
27. Hibernian F.C., a Scottish First Division football club, were privileged to have subsequent Neste Oy Trading Manager, Ron Gray, wearing the green No. 1 shirt.

28. According to sources, this was believed to have been the wily but well -liked Welshman, Player Edwards.
29. Europ-Oil Prices: 13/04/1984, p. 1.
30. Attributable to Rod Gavshon, a popular ex Conoco, Neste and Vitol senior trader.
31. Wolmar, C. Obituary of Sir Alistair Morton Guardian newspaper 03/09/2004.
32. Lord Simon became CEO and Chairman of BP during the 1990s and Conn went on to become CEO of Centrica. There are many other examples amongst them Andy Duff who led National Power and chaired Thames Water, Tufan Erginbilgic, CEO of Rolls Royce and Bryan Sanderson, a Chairman of Standard Chartered Bank.

BIBLIOGRAPHY

Ammann, Daniel (2009): The King of Oil : The Secret Lives of Marc Rich, St Martin's Press.

Argus Media: Weekly Petroleum Argus, Various Issues.

Atkinson, F. and Hall, S. (2016): Oil and the British Economy, Routledge.

Bryce, C.D.S. (2020): London Trading's Good Old Days, PE Media 23/7/20–3/8/20.

Harvie, Christopher (1994): Fools Gold The Story of North Sea Oil, Hamish Hamilton.

Hoopes Stephanie, M. (1994): The Privatisation of UK Oil Assets 1977–1987 LSE PhD Thesis.

Horsnell, P. and Mabro (1993): Oil Markets and Prices, Oxford University Press.

Hurt, Harry (1984): Feasting on the Oil Glut Texas Monthly October.

Kemp, A. (2012): The Official History of North Sea Oil and Gas Vols 1 and 2, Routledge.

Mabro et al. (1986): The Market for North Sea Crude Oil, Oxford University Press.

McGraw Hill PIW, Various Issues.

Morrison, K. (2008): Living in a Material World, Wiley.

Norman James, R. (1995): Oilman, Trader, Banker Spy, Forbes Magazine 30/01/95.

Shepherd, M. (2015): Oil Strike North Sea, Luath Press.

CHAPTER 5

Brent Legacy

Kurt Chapman

Abstract As the Brent market developed and grew, so did the number of related instruments such as, 'exchange of futures for physical' (EFP), 'contracts for difference' (CFD), 'dated to frontline' (DFL) and many others. New brokers and companies entered the market, adding interesting individuals and the colour of their corporate cultures. Traders assumed the role of storing oil. All of this and much more will be described by a former global head of oil of Mercuria, one of the biggest trading companies.

Keywords Futures · Swaps · EFP · Traders · Operational tolerance · Tax spinning

K. Chapman (✉)
London, UK
e-mail: kurtjohnchapman@gmail.com

© The Author(s), under exclusive license to Springer Nature Switzerland AG 2023
A. Imsirovic (ed.), *Brent Crude Oil*,
https://doi.org/10.1007/978-3-031-28232-4_5

59

HEATHER AND BRENT PARTIALS

My interest in commodities and ultimate passion with Brent began when my family moved to London in 1981, around the time I entered Harvard University to study economics. My father, John Chapman, had taken on the role of marketing the Union Oil Company of California's (Unocal).[1] North Sea oil production. One of their fields was Heather,[2] part of the Ninian system. Since late 1978, daily production had been about 10,000 barrels.

At that time, the Brent forward market was in its infancy and traded basis full cargoes of 600,000 barrels. Dad became one of the first to engage in the use of Brent partials. A partial market of 100,000 barrel increments suited the hedging needs of Unocal. He engaged with Colin Bryce[3] at Morgan Stanley, developing a suitable contract that allowed for the trading of this new instrument. Ultimately, Brent partials would evolve into the International Petroleum Exchange (IPE) Brent future contract in 1988.

The ownership of the Heather field would eventually pass to EnQuest.[4] By 2017, I was purchasing the Heather oil production on behalf of Mercuria as part of a prefinancing deal and aggregating the volume to make full Brent cargoes. Sadly, the Heather field has now shut but its lifetime dovetails fondly with the Chapman family Brent trading experience.

ALL ROADS LEAD TO BRENT

I joined Morgan Stanley in New York in 1989 after a four-year stint in the United States Marine Corps. Most of my university buddies were on Wall Street and I had caught the financial bug. My father helped open a few doors and I secured an entry level position at this emerging 'Wall Street refiner'. I started off position keeping, executing futures and market making in cash WTI (West Texas Intermediate crude oil traded at Cushing, Oklahoma).

Six months later a position opened in the London office. I jumped at the chance to relocate and work for Colin Bryce! In London, I continued over the counter (OTC) market making, expanding into all three global benchmarks—WTI, Brent and Dubai. Shell UK was one of my largest clients. They didn't want to be seen trading WTI, so we provided them with an OTC Brent partial that was priced basis the New York Mercantile Exchange (NYMEX).

In 1990, Transnor, a Bermuda-based trading company filed a complaint in U.S. Federal court alleging several oil majors including Shell, BP and Exxon had colluded in setting the price of Brent thus leading to Transnor's losses during 1986. In my opinion, the majors were engaged in tax spinning. In reality, the price collapse was due to the Saudis introducing 'net back' crude oil pricing in order to regain their market share.[5]

The court ruled that because the Brent market was 'primarily' a futures contract the suit could go ahead. The claim, however, was settled out of court, so the ruling was never clarified. As participants in the Brent forward trading market shunned U.S.-based entities, Morgan Stanley and others set up foreign entities, mainly based in London, in order to work around what became an informal ban on trading Brent from the United States.

Overnight, I became the 'go to' Brent executor inside our company—unknowingly setting my career on a path that would remain intrinsically linked to Brent for its duration.

Most Brent and Dubai partials were traded versus WTI as NYMEX had been the most liquid oil futures contract since 1983. That was changing with the emergence of a successful Brent futures contract in 1988. The IPE allowed off-exchange futures trading through a mechanism known as the 'two-sided' Exchange of Futures for Physical (EFP). For example, Company A buys a 100,000 barrel August Brent partial from Company B. Then Company A sells the same 100,000 barrel August Brent partial back to Company B on an EFP basis, posting 100 lots of August Brent futures. The OTC partials transactions netted out to zero. Company A was left long 100 August Brent futures while Company B was correspondingly short the 100 lots.

Eventually, the introduction of 'block trades' (bilateral trades of blocks of 100 contracts, at market price, posted on the exchange) superseded the two-sided EFP. It was much easier to transact and a lot less paperwork!

Robin Bieber, an oil broker with Amerex, had a very active client from South Africa that wanted the anonymity that came with trading futures, but also the liquidity provided by the Brent partial contract. Robin actively promoted the use of this mechanism and helped build volume on the exchange by 'crossing' these partial transactions. It also allowed Amerex to maintain a decent brokerage commission.

On August 2, 1990, I received a very early morning call at home in London from our Asian team. 'Get in the office, Iraq has invaded Kuwait!' As I sat on the empty trading floor, phones started lighting up. The market was gapping higher. Feeling I should take some action, I called Colin Bryce. 'Buy something!' was his response. 'In this situation you need to be long'. So, I bought a 15-day Brent at $20.95 per barrel from Statoil, fretting that having paid $4 per barrel higher than the previous days close, it would be a losing trade. I needn't have worried as the market continues to rally for months.

The first Gulf War saw Brent futures activity explode. With the increased volumes, it was not uncommon to see different prices being traded on opposite sides of the 'open outcry' pit. On any given day I may have used five or six brokers—Amerex, Credit Lyonnais Rouse, ED&F Man, GNI, Sabex and Trafalgar. Each broker had their own special clients, and the volumes would be 'shopped' around so they could capture both sides of a transaction.

In 2001, the Intercontinental Exchange (ICE) acquired the IPE and by 2005 the trading floor closed when the contract went electronic.[6] Some of those brokers migrated 'upstairs' to transact oil derivatives but many of them simply ceased operation.

Physical, Forward and Futures Brent

I left Morgan Stanley in 1991 and joined Elf Trading in Geneva. I desired exposure to physical crude oil trading while contributing to Elf's expanding presence in the paper[7] markets. Elf had a large portfolio of West African and North Sea oil production, and all of the pricing exposure was hedged using the Brent forward contract. The commingling of the Brent and Ninian fields had recently occurred and a standardised 15-day forward contract was codified under Shell UK 1990 general terms and conditions. Cargo size had been reduced to 500,000 barrels but the five per cent tolerance in buyer's option was maintained. Nominations had to be passed by 5 o'clock London time, 15 days (hence the name) prior to the first day of a three day loading laycan at Sullom Voe Terminal, Shetland Islands, Scotland.

Brent trading was going full guns. The major UK North Sea production companies (Shell, BP and Exxon) had a huge incentive to sell their Brent equity in advance (using the 15-day Brent contract). If prices fell in the subsequent two days (reduced to one day in 1993) they would buy back their sale and declare a corporate trading profit. Conversely, if the market price rose, they would declare the sale to the tax authorities and pay the higher Petroleum Revenue Tax (PRT). This was called 'tax spinning'.[8] It was honed to a fine art by BP using Monte Carlo simulations while Shell and Exxon had their own methods. But in all cases, the majors were sellers every day. Most mornings, I would sell futures in anticipation of being able to buy back a 15-day Brent from the producers resulting in a long EFP position.[9] Little did I know that owning EFPs would become a huge profit opportunity in a few years' time.

Declining production in the older oil fields subject to the Price Reference Tax (PRT), a reduction in the tax (repealed in 2016), and the introduction of a supplemental charge in 2002 meant that 'tax spinning' eventually lost most of its incentive.

Just as with the futures market community, having multiple relationships with the OTC brokers (Amerex, Fearnoil, First National, PVM, Spectron and United) was important. The broker PVM had developed a strong relationship with the Japanese trading houses. Kanematsu, in particular, had embarked on a systematic trading style that led to them holding a significant long 15-day Brent position, rumoured to be up to 40 cargoes. They were also day trading in and out of their position providing liquidity to the 'tax spinners'.

Kanematsu did not intend to take their long forward position to physical delivery. So, at the end of a trading month, the position was rolled to the subsequent month. This was done by selling Brent spreads. Similar activity was also occurring on the IPE. Several funds would accumulate long positions and then need to sell the spread between the front two contracts to 'roll' their positions. The impact on the spread value was short term but profound.

Eventually, as hedge funds came to dominate flat price trading, the oil industry participants retreated to trading the spreads. Funds express their view on the market in absolute price, reflecting their global macroeconomic opinion. On the other hand, oil traders see a particular type of crude oil or maturity in relative value terms, trading time spreads and geographical arbitrages (WTI versus Brent and Brent versus Dubai).

Physical cargoes are hedged using the Brent forward or futures contracts, but the barrels are actually priced off the assessment for Dated Brent, normally the five quoted days after the bill of lading (B/L) date or in some cases the average of all the quotations during the month of loading. Not long after the introduction of the Brent forward market, the price reporting agencies (PRA) Platts (now S&P Global Commodities Insights) and Petroleum Argus (now Argus Media) began publishing a daily Dated Brent assessment in 1987 reflecting the prompt value of physical Brent cargoes.[10]

Since Brent crude was freely traded[11] on a spot basis in the Atlantic Basin, participants deemed it a 'fair' value for their crude oil. Supported by some national oil companies such as the Nigerian National Petroleum Corporation (NNPC), the Dated Brent assessment became the industry's benchmark. Today, a majority of the world's crude oil production is priced at a differential to Platts Dated Brent including North Sea, West African, Mediterranean, Russian and Brazilian grades.

DERIVATIVE BRENT CONTRACTS

While the differential between Dated Brent and other grades (such as Ekofisk, Bonny Light, Urals) is usually fixed at the time of trading, the differential between Dated Brent pricing and Forward Brent hedging floats and can be volatile. The introduction of a financial instrument known as contract for difference (CFD) addressed the issue. Emanating from the gold markets as a way to capture price movements without the cost of physical exposure, a CFD could be traded at a fixed differential between the two Brents and then unwound over an agreed pricing period. The swap then settled financially. Maturities quickly standardised in calendar weeks as this five day period was generally in line with physical pricing. The early providers of this swap were trading companies Transworld Oil and Louis Dreyfus, promoted by United broking. Soon, other dated swaps were also introduced to facilitate price management against Brent futures, notably monthly average Dated Brent to frontline IPE Brent settlement (DFL).

Leaving Elf in 1994, I moved back to London to work for the U.S. refiner Ashland (now part of Marathon). I marketed their Nigerian production of Antan and Brass River crude oil, while occasionally using the CFDs to align the different purchase and sale pricing exposures.

More importantly, I was charged with optimising the refinery crude slate, replacing the usual refinery diet of Louisiana Light Sweet (LLS) with cheaper foreign alternatives. Ashland was a regular customer of BP and Phibro as they were both looking for outlets of physical Brent and Forties to complement their North Sea trading positions. On several occasions I negotiated the purchase of two million barrels of Brent or Forties to be delivered on a very large crude carrier (VLCC) to the Louisiana Offshore Oil Port (LOOP). A particularly memorable deal was struck with Malcom McAvity of Phibro[12] for two VLCCs of Brent versus LLS. It turned out to be some of the cheapest North Sea oil to ever land in the U.S. Gulf. After discharging at LOOP, the crude was pumped up Capline Pipeline[13] to the Ashland refinery at Catlettsburg, Kentucky.

Working at Ashland gave me great exposure to physical crude oil trading in the Atlantic Basin, but I wanted to do more in the paper markets. In 1996, I accepted a trading position at Koch Supply and Trading in London. My focus shifted to optimising the five per cent buyer's tolerance option embedded in the 15-day Brent contract.[14] Phibro and later BP capitalised on this aspect during periods of increased flat price volatility.

OPERATIONAL TOLERANCE AND BRENT 'CHAINS'

Operational tolerance was captured during the 15-day Brent nomination procedure. As cargoes passed from one counterparty to another, a 'daisy chain' or simply 'chains' would be established. The more buys 'ins' and sales 'outs' you had, the greater number of times you would be in the chains. The price levels of the purchases and sales drove tolerance profit. For example, if you had a purchase from Exxon at $15.00 and a sale to Vitol at $16.00, your exposure was $1 per barrel.

Cargoes have a parcel number generated by the terminal operator such as 'B0101'; 'B' for Brent, '01' for the month of January and then '01' if the cargo was the first cargo of the programme. When passing a nomination, you would receive a 'B0101' cargo, loading January 1–3, purchased at $15.00 from Exxon. You would then declare the same 'B0101' Brent cargo to Vitol at $16.00. The 'keeper' of the cargo by 5 o'clock could then exercise the five per cent tolerance option when loading or selling it on as a Dated Brent cargo. If the cargo loaded as a 525,000 barrel 'max' parcel, you would gain $25,000. If the cargo loaded as a 475,000 barrel 'min' parcel, you lost $25,000.

The trick was to 'wrap' as much tolerance as possible into the chain while constructing it in a way that the cargo would come back to you for keeping. It was not unusual to build $10 of tolerance, a potential profit or loss of half a million dollars.[15] Good 15-day Brent operators understood this commercial aspect of their job. Steve Begg at BP went on to become one of the outstanding Brent traders of my time and parlayed his experience successfully not only at BP and but also later with trading houses Trafigura and Glencore.

The consequence of tolerance meant that 15-day Brent traded at a premium to Dated Brent. This was known as the 'cost of keeping' or the value you would lose by converting a forward purchase into a Dated cargo. The tolerance gained should compensate for that cost. The flip side of trading forward Brent was the risk of 'clocking'. As the cost of keeping grew, the probability of ending up with an unwanted cargo increased. Nominations were passed from the producer, down the chain until someone kept the cargo. If no one was willing to keep, the 'music stopped' at 5 o'clock London time. If you couldn't pass in time, you owned the cargo, usually at a loss.[16]

To avoid these losses, elaborate systems were developed to ensure the passing of nominations with maximum speed and efficiency. One operator would handle the 'hotline' for incoming calls. The others would be on standby ready to speed dial out and declare the nomination. In the background an atomic clock would be counting down the seconds on speaker. Often, we went to 'the tapes' to see if nominations had beaten the deadline. It could be a surreal, doomsday scenario evoking both elation and disappointment. At Koch, we were once clocked twice on the same day with both cargoes coming from Phibro in the last seconds!

PLATTS WINDOW

The Platts 'window' proved to be the busiest period of the OTC trading day. This was when the reporting agency would assess the value of both Dated Brent and 15-day Brent, the latter on a weighted average basis. Initially, the window was 45 minutes long and commenced after the exchange contracts had settled. During my stint at Elf in Geneva, that was 9:45 to 10:30 p.m.! I would likely be at a local restaurant with a large portable phone in hand, scribbling trades on a paper tablecloth. Later, the window was reduced to 30 minutes but the weighted average methodology[17] still meant that trading accelerated rapidly towards the end of the period.

One evening, while I was hedging Koch's pricing exposure, it all kicked off. Danny Masters of JPMorgan was a large buyer of front month 15-day Brent cargoes. On the other side, Tom Ross of BP was a large seller of the second month but in clips of 500,000 partials for EFP. BP was adamant about not selling cash in order to maintain a long EFP position.

As Danny bought more cash, Tom sold more futures. Ultimately, BP sold the equivalent of 12 Brent cargoes (6 million barrels) while JPMorgan managed to buy a 13th forward Brent cargo, for a total of 6.5 million barrels. The spread between the two months blew out to levels 30 cents over the value trading 'on the screen' (in futures markets). I found myself selling to JPMorgan and buying from BP and then buying the spread on the IPE. I repeated the trade four times in less than 10 minutes and amazingly added $500,000 to our profit. Not bad for a late night in the office!

Originally, Platts editors manually published relevant price information on Platts Global Alert (known as page 3). By 2008, Platts launched their eWindow platform on ICE for electronic Brent partial trading. The window is still 30 minutes long, but the process has moved to a market on close (MOC) assessment. In essence, the last repeatable trade sets the quote. Traders also post their own bids and offers for CFDs and physical cargoes. The technology has vastly improved the accuracy of data collection to aid in assessment.

PURE BRENT TRADING

I moved into a pure trading role at Sempra Energy Trading in early 1999. Marco Dunand and Daniel Jaeggi had left Phibro to start Sempra's international crude oil business and invited me on board. It was a serious step up in both the taking and the understanding of risk.

While being long the Brent EFP allowed you to capture tolerance, being short the EFP led to another trading opportunity. By 'going to expiry',[18] one could cover a short forward Brent position while benefiting from the underlying long futures position.

The Brent Index is the basis for financially settling the Brent futures contract.[19] It combines the weighted average of three elements; outright Brent forward trades in the prompt month, outright trades in the second month plus the Brent spread trades between the prompt versus second month, and assessments by PRAs. The independent assessments are taken at specific times during the expiry day and were initially provided by London Oil Reports (now Independent Commodity Intelligence Services or ICIS), Petroleum Argus, Platts, Reuters, RIM, Telerate Dow Jones and eventually Bloomberg. Over time, all but one PRA withdrew from the process. It is a credit to Tony Dillon, former managing editor, that ICIS is still contributing. His diligence and integrity were highly respected.

As the importance of the Brent Benchmark grew, the Brent Index would become more tightly defined due to both industry and regulatory pressure. A revised method to calculate the Brent index was introduced for the November 2018 contract. The main components remain the same but there is an increased reliance on futures trades to derive their own index. ICE 'minute marker' contract settlements plus an EFP premium have been incorporated while Brent Forward and spread trades are concentrated into designated 30-minute assessment windows.

In the decade following the 1990 commingling of the Brent and Ninian systems, the number of Brent cargoes per month had fallen from over 50 to 20. The decline became apparent in August 2000 when Arcadia and Glencore amassed long positions in the Dated Brent swap market, complementing existing Dated Brent positions emanating from physical oil. Brent cargoes were uniquely sold to India and also moved into storage at Saldanha Bay near Cape Town, South Africa. The Brent quote was bid to over Dated Brent plus $3 and remained unchanged for several weeks!

The following year, responding to the need for greater physical liquidity, Platts began accepting offers from ship-to-ship (STS) transfers into their assessment method. Large vessels would load at Sullom Voe and then move to Scapa Flow, Scotland. From there a Dated Brent cargo could be offered and if sold, reverse lightered on to a small vessel, usually an Aframax with at least a 600,000 barrel capacity. Yet later that same year, BP still cornered the November 2001 15-day Brent market. The U.S. Strategic Petroleum Reserve (SPR) had earlier released 30 million barrels of oil to be refilled. BP managed to secure several of the contracts, kept the majority of the Brent programme and resupplied the oil.

The coup de grace, however, came in February 2002. Sempra Energy Trading sold five VLCCs of Brent to Sinochem for delivery into China. The intention was to convert a long futures position into cash, exercise the tolerance and fulfil the commitment. The February/March Brent spread moved from flat (zero) to over $1. As is invariably the case, someone else was on the other side. Ultimately a huge EFP roll (February/March 15-day Brent versus February/March Brent futures) of 34 cargoes and 17,000 contracts was agreed between BP and Sempra on expiry day to square positions.

By July 2002, the original 15-day Brent contract was no more. Forties and Oseberg were added, cargo size reverted back to 600,000 barrels and the nomination period was extended. The new contract became

21-day BFO (Brent/Forties/Oseberg) and the Brent contractual terms (Shell UK General Terms and Conditions, popularly known as SUKO GT&Cs) were modified. Significantly, the buyer's tolerance option was reduced from five to one per cent. So, instead of plus or minus 25,000 barrels, it was now only 6,000 barrels. The construction of the Dated Brent assessment also gained a new dimension. The widened nomination period meant cargoes were now evaluated from 10 to 21 days forward (23 days on a Friday) instead of 7–15 days. Therefore, the market structure expressed by the weekly CFD curve became more relevant. 3–6 days added another week of dated value into the process. The quote had been derived from week one CFD. Now it would include both week one and week two.

Spearheaded by Jorge Montepeque at Platts, these radical changes would transform Brent into the most complex commodities benchmark and contribute to the growth of all the instruments that make up the Brent complex.[20] It also took the steam out of the tolerance game associated with leveraging Forward Brent and shifted the focus towards the trading of Dated Brent swaps.

All subsequent North Sea crude oil additions to the Brent Forward contract have been based on the view that the underlying production levels should be maintained above 800,000 barrels per day. Ekofisk was added in 2007 making the contract BFOE. In another development, the Buzzard field was injected into Forties changing the nature of the blend from sweet to sour. A sulphur de-escalator was introduced to compensate buyers for sulphur content over 0.6 per cent. However, from then on Forties became the marginal barrel. In January 2012, the contract was extended further to 25 days.

MARKET CHANGES

I transitioned to Mercuria Energy Trading in 2006, a few years after my bosses at Sempra had left to form this new business with a Polish-based Russian Urals trader. The commercial relationship with J&S Group had been long standing and we were providing them with Dated Brent swaps to hedge monthly flows of crude oil through the northern Druzhba pipeline. In addition, we initiated the sale of Urals to China via the port of Gdansk. Volumes of Urals could be as high as 5 million barrels per month.

We expanded the swaps business by offering it to other producers with similar profiles. TNK-BP[21] and Surgutneftegas[22] became large clients for a period of time. The oil market moved into a steep contango by year end. We had leased two of the six 7.5 million barrel concrete storage tanks at the Strategic Fuel Fund Association (SFF) in Saldanha Bay. It allowed us to purchase distressed[23] crude oil from the entire Atlantic Basin. Almost all of these barrels were priced off Dated Brent. Some of the crude oil stored there was even part of the Brent 'basket'. We surprised Norsk Hydro in the Platts window by purchasing an Oseberg that travelled to Saldanha Bay solo on an Aframax. Several Ekofisk Suezmax tankers (1MM barrels) followed years later. The Dated Brent was converted to Brent futures using swaps and EFPs or Mean of Platts (MOP) so that the Brent spread hedges could be easily managed using futures markets.

It was a straightforward calculation to determine the cost of carry-storage rental, financing and insurance for losses. The finesse came when deciding in which month to place hedges. That would depend on your medium to long term (3 months to 2 years) view on market structure plus the length of the storage contract. When the market eventually flipped into backwardation, we sold the oil mainly to Asia and unwound the hedges by selling Brent spreads. Saldanha was not our only storage location. We also held close to three million barrels of mainly Brent and Forties but also Urals in Nord-West Oelleitung's (NWO) salt caverns near Wilhelmshaven, Germany. These contango trading opportunities reoccurred in 2009–2011 after the Global Financial Crisis and again in 2014–2016 when the Saudis decided to take on the U.S. shale oil producers in a battle for market share.

In 2011, the European Union (EU) signed a Free Trade Agreement (FTA) with South Korea reducing tariffs on some imported goods. The consequence was a three per cent reduction in the price of North Sea crude oil moving there. With the oil price at $100 per barrel, the discount was enough to cover the cost of freight to Korea. BP was the first to act and in December 2011 they loaded a VLCC of Forties at Hound Point, Scotland, destination Korea. They were quickly followed by Vitol, Shell and Chevron (who had a joint venture with GS Energy, named GS-Caltex, in a refinery at Yeosu). Statoil was also able to capitalise on the FTA, Norway being a member of the European Economic Area (EEA). They began loading VLCCs of Troll from Mongstad for Korean customers.

Throughout 2012, every month two VLCCs of crude oil underpinning the Dated Brent market were moving to Korea.[24] With the flat price decline in 2014, an additional market structure incentive was needed. The 45-day passage from the North Sea to Korea during the severe contango helped finance this trade. In fact, traders would often load a VLCC of Forties and anchor the vessel off Southwold, England. The contango covered the cost of the 'floating storage' and the lifters had the option to reoffer the barrels into the Platts window via STS if the barrels couldn't be placed East.

Another game changer was the lifting of the export ban on U.S. crude in early 2016. The rise of U.S. shale oil production and the restriction on its sale for domestic use led to a huge discount of WTI relative to Brent. The differential had reached extremes of more than $30 per barrel. Producers were desperate to achieve international crude oil prices and began exploring loopholes in the regulations to move small amounts of condensate to foreign destinations. Ultimately this pressured the U.S. government to overturn the 40-year-old legislation enacted after the 1973 oil crisis.[25] Exports of U.S. domestic crude oil (primarily WTI Midland) have steadily climbed ever since and import volumes have overtaken the production level of the Brent 'basket' (even with Troll having been added in 2018 to make the Brent Forward BFOET). WTI Midland has become the preferred U.S. grade with refiners due to its higher quality than WTI Cushing, while also being logistically easier to export with dedicated pipelines moving the oil directly from West Texas to the U.S. Gulf Coast.

FINANCIALISATON

After the 2008 financial crisis, legislation was introduced that dramatically impacted the Dated Brent swap markets by forcing industry participants to put their activity onto a regulated exchange.[26] Dated swaps at that time were generally traded through OTC brokers with the buyer and seller assuming each other's credit exposure. An exchange of futures for swaps (EFS) mechanism existed for swaps to be cleared on ICE but that was usually only done to mitigate credit risk with smaller counterparties. By 2012, ICE announced the listing of over 300 new oil swap futures contracts.

Dated swaps became futures and could be easily traded or 'blocked' on the exchange. Producers and end users gained access to instruments traditionally dominated by banks, trading houses and majors. Pure financial liquidity providers (so called 'curve strippers') like Mandara, Onyx and DV Trading started to influence the value of the North Sea Dated Strip, one of the three components of the Dated Brent assessment. The other two components remained in the domain of physical traders, the physical premium of a Brent 'basket' crude oil to Dated Brent and the absolute value of the Brent Forward as traded by partials. When arbitraging monthly DFL versus weekly CFDs, the strippers tried to capture the dislocations that can occur between the two instruments by buying one and selling the other. The resulting synthetic EFP position (forward from CFD and futures from DFL) that priced out over the maturity of the swaps was then managed efficiently using the MOP and trade at settlement (TAS).

Banks like Morgan Stanley, JPMorgan and Barclays exited the trading space due to higher capital requirements and directives to focus on core business rather than proprietary trading. In addition, central banks moved interest rates dramatically lower to stabilise the financial system. Money was cheap. Trade financing shifted from the commercial banks of BNP Paribas and ING to the trading houses of Glencore, Trafigura and Vitol.

CONVERGENCE

While the addition of Forties, Oseberg and Ekofisk into Brent Forward (BFOE) increased contract volumes, a discrepancy in quality remained. Oseberg and Ekofisk have a consistently higher refining value and trade at a significant premium to Dated Brent. It became more apparent over time that Forties was always setting the Dated Brent quote, even with the help of the sulphur de-escalator. Narrowing the gap between Forties and the other grades was an opportunity for another profitable trading strategy. If you could place a large portion of Forties to local refiners and Korea, then any BFOE positions would rally to the level where producers were willing to sell their Oseberg and Ekofisk.

In late 2012, we saw that Dated Brent swaps and BFOE were very close in price. It gave us a chance to go long the December/January Brent spread and short CFDs (Dated Brent to January) at a very small discount. We ultimately managed to accumulate 44 December BFOE cargoes, quietly collecting Brent partials in the window and converting them into cargoes. On the day prior to the expiry, we bought several more spreads, two being from ConocoPhillips at $1.20 per barrel. The next morning ConocoPhillips bought back both spreads at $1.55 realising that they had sold their Ekofisk production cheap. We continued to sell Brent spreads at similar levels over the course of the day until the shorts had covered Oseberg and Ekofisk forwards. This left us long the entire December Forties programme, but we were hedged. We assumed that we would be offering the cargoes for the next month. As it turned out, Shell was interested in the oil for both refining and trading purposes. We sold the barrels at a Dated Brent premium, effectively covering the short hedges and moved on!

In July 2013, Platts introduced quality premiums (QPs) to compensate sellers who nominated Oseberg and Ekofisk in the Brent chains.[27] After their introduction, Oseberg and particularly Ekofisk would set the Dated Brent quote more frequently. There continued to be small distortions, but this additional mechanism helped balance the quality discrepancies of the Brent basket of crude oil.

Theoretically, the Brent complex works on the principle that over time the value of its components become one or converge. If you bought a 15-day Brent and held the contract, you would ultimately receive a Dated Brent cargo in the same month of maturity. As the forward market moved from 15-day, 21-day, 25-day and finally to one full month ahead in February 2015, the futures market remained based on the original 15-day window. Dislocations between the Dated Brent, Brent Forward and Brent futures increased. There were fewer forward cargoes eligible for the Brent index and Brent futures prices soared relative to the rest of the complex.

In a contango market, the EFP went negative as players tried to avoid ending up with first half of the programme cargoes. Position limits were introduced by ICE to temper speculative influences but with liberal exemptions granted, they were only marginally effective. Finally, the exchange recognised the need to adapt but this was not to happen before the March 2016 contract. In the interim, there was a massive 'convergence' trading opportunity. Dated Brent swaps were trading $1 under Brent futures. At Mercuria, we were a steady buyer of calendar year 2016 DFL swaps acquiring over 4 million barrels per month, 50 million barrels in total. We sold the Brent futures spread strip to align the two parts of the instrument. This made us long Dated Brent and short Brent futures of the same maturities. We then rolled the back end of the position into the first half of the year. These were the months that would be most impacted by the forthcoming change in the ICE futures contract. The convergence happened quickly. The EFP moved from minus 35 cents per barrel to zero and Dated Brent strengthened by a similar amount. Inevitably, we didn't get out of the whole position and gave back a portion of our profit, but it certainly turned out to be one of my best trades.

PRIVILEGE

I am privileged to have had a career in such a dynamic industry, especially trading the Brent market. The friendships I forged continue to this day. One such relationship is with a terminal operator, Zenith Energy.[28] In 2015, Zenith acquired a storage facility at Bantry Bay, Ireland, from Phillips 66. At their request, I turned up with two Forties cargoes and signed a two year deal to occupy the majority of their spare capacity. After my retirement from Mercuria, Zenith asked me to join their board as an independent director. Later, when my son, Jake, graduated from university, he joined the company as a project engineer. Who knows? Perhaps Jake will be the third generation Chapman to trade 'Brent'!

NOTES

1. Unocal was a petroleum explorer and marketer based in California. It merged with Chevron in 2005.
2. https://www.lyellcollection.org/doi/abs/10.1144/gsl.mem.2003.020. 01.25.
3. Colin Bryce has written a chapter in this book.
4. EnQuest is an independent oil and gas production and company. See https://www.enquest.com.
5. For details, see the chapter by Adi Imsirovic.
6. See the chapter by David Peniket, former president of ICE Futures Europe.
7. Paper oil normally refers to the futures, options and swaps trading.
8. For more details, see the chapter by Liz Bossley.
9. Long 500,000 barrels of 15-day Brent and short 500 lots of Brent futures in the same maturity.
10. For the role of PRAs, see the chapter by Adrian Binks and Neil Fleming.
11. There are no restrictions on resale or destinations as is the case for many Middle East crudes.
12. Malcom was a Vice Chairman of Phibro LLC, one of the world's leading international commodities trading firms, from 1986 to 2012. https://www.macroaxis.com/invest/manager/LPG/Malcolm-McAvity.
13. The flow was reversed in 2021. https://www.marathonpipeline.com/Cap line/.

14. The final buyer of the forward contract had the option to increase or reduce the volume of the full Brent cargo by five per cent. See the chapter by David Godfrey.

15. If you kept the cargo, you gained $250,000. But if someone else kept it and turned the tolerance against you, you lost that amount, hence $500,000 ($250,000 plus $250,000).

16. 'Clocking' was common in contango markets when the prompt cargoes were trading below physical for later delivery.

17. The 'window' is designed like a funnel. Early bids and offers were wide. They would get closer and closer, until Brent partials began trading. The final price was set based on the weighted average of the trades.

18. Keeping the short position until the very last day when the index settlement of the Brent contract on the exchange is determined.

19. https://www.theice.com/futures-europe/brent.

20. The Brent complex includes not only physical cargoes but also forwards, futures, options and a plethora of swaps such as CFDs and DFLs.

21. A joint venture between the Russian oil company Tyumenskaya Neftyanaya Kompaniya (Tyumen Oil Company) and BP which was acquired by Rosneft in 2013.

22. https://www.surgutneftegas.ru/en/.

23. Crude oil which is difficult to sell due to the lack of demand.

24. Bloomberg, 'Supertankers of North Sea Crude Shipped to South Korea' published 7 September 2012.

25. https://www.congress.gov/bill/114th-congress/house-bill/2029.

26. The Dodd-Frank Wall Street Reform and Consumer Protection Act was signed in 2010.

27. https://www.spglobal.com/commodityinsights/plattscontent/_assets/_files/en/our-methodology/methodology-specifications/emea-crude-methodology.pdf.

28. https://www.zenithterminals.com/.

CHAPTER 6

Brent Crude Oil Trading operations—The Rise and Fall of 'Clocking'

David Godfrey

Abstract This chapter explains why the Brent operations are very different from the operations of other oil contracts. The nomination procedure, from seller to the buyer and with a sharp deadline for passing the nominations at five a clock London time, created such pressures on the operators that multiple phone lines and atomic clocks were used to avoid the infamous 'clocking', a situation in which a nomination could not be passed on to another buyer and large financial loss was almost guaranteed. With each physical Brent cargo trading many times, the resulting

---

Clocking is a term used by market players when the nomination from the seller to the buyer could not be passed any further down the Brent chain, due to the contractual time limitation of five o'clock in the afternoon, London time. It is described in detail in this chapter.

D. Godfrey (✉)
Retired, Folkestone, England
e-mail: davidgodfrey@hawkinge-tc.gov.uk; david.r.godfrey@btinternet.com

© The Author(s), under exclusive license to Springer Nature
Switzerland AG 2023
A. Imsirovic (ed.), *Brent Crude Oil*,
https://doi.org/10.1007/978-3-031-28232-4_6

'daisy chains' created headaches for the operators as the full set of documents, issued once the physical cargo has loaded took many months and
even years to through the trade chain (including banks) to reach the end
receiver. This resulted in extensive use of the letters of indemnity (LOIs),
which unfortunately, could lead to lengthy and costly legal actions.

Keywords Clocking · Brent chains · Daisy chains · Letter of indemnity

Back in the 1983, the daily routine of many trading operations teams
changed dramatically when some of their Traders developed a new trading
tool for forward 'over the counter' (OTC) Brent blend crude oil deliv-
eries at the Sullom Voe Terminal in the Shetland Islands. They called it
15-day Brent and introduced terms[1] such as backwardation,[2] contango,[3]
partials and top-ups,[4] all of which changed life in the oil operations teams
dramatically.

At that time, I was the manager of crude oil operations for British
National Oil Corporation (BNOC), working alongside some of the co-
authors of this book.[5]

We were a young and enthusiastic team who until then had been used
to a fairly stable routine based on traditional 'term' deal trading arrangements, involving sorting out the logistics of physical oil flow at loading
terminals.

The BNOC was dissolved in 1985 and I was recruited by the wily
old French fox Bernard de Combret who set up Elf Trading S.A. in
Geneva[6] in order to be free of the Bureaucracy of the Elf Head Office
in La Défense, Paris. My role as General Manager Trading Operations of
Elf Trading SA (ETSA) was to build a new operations team to support
the newly formed trading team under the charismatic and capable Nicolas
Fresnau. In the 1980s, ETSA became a major player in the Brent 15-day
market and following a merger with Total, it become Total Trading S.A
(Totsa). In 2021 the Total group rebranded itself as TotalEnergies.

History

It is worth stepping back in time to the origins of the story when crude oil
was first delivered into the Sullom Voe Oil Terminal in 1978. There were
two main oil pipelines feeding into the Sullom Voe Terminal; the Brent

pipeline operated by Shell and the Ninian pipeline operated by BP. First oil from the Dunlin field, part of the Brent system connecting to the Brent pipeline arrived in November 1978, followed by a cargo of Ninian, in December 1978. Both pipeline systems gathered oil from several offshore oil fields, with more in the 'pipeline', so to speak.

Fortunately, being a simple operations person, I just had to manage my team to focus on terminal operations. In a nutshell, our task was to gather production forecasts entitlements from the producing fields, ascertain total expected throughput and allocate them in accordance with the producers' equity shares of the respective oil fields. Having calculated each producer's available quantities for the month, the producer was then obligated to nominate preferred three-day date ranges within which buyers would charter oil tankers to take away their entitlements. The final allocation of loading date ranges which needed to be spread evenly through the month was governed by a set of rules using a simple credit and debit principles, governed by the Sullom Voe Terminal Operating Agreement between Shell UK Ltd and BP Petroleum Development, dated 19 March 1979.

Put simply, each producer had a 'bank' account into which its daily production accrued until such time as sufficient volumes were forecast to be accrued to make a cargos size withdrawal. Large volume producers would reach these levels very quickly. However, smaller producers might have to wait for a full month's accrual, and an 'overdraft' facility was available for them to be treated equitably. Conversely, no one was permitted to stockpile to the extent that throughput of the terminal might be jeopardised.

In practice, many of the smaller producers entered into long-term arrangements to sell their equity production to the larger players, to make life easier for them and to ensure a smoother financial returns, without having to worry about the logistics and market fluctuations.

As a result of these processes a monthly lifting programme was established, setting out cargo quantities and a 3-day loading window known as 'laydays'. These were marked as 'TBN' ('to be nominated') until such time as a named tanker was fixed.

At its peak, the total daily throughput of Brent Blend Crude Oil at Sullom Voe was almost 1.5 million barrels per day,[7] and it was loaded onto tankers ranging in size from so-called LR1 45–80,000 dead-weight tonnes (DWT, approximately 375,000–600,000 barrels) to very large crude carriers (or VLCCs of 160–320 DWT, approximately 1,200,000–2,400,000 barrels).

Any shipping operator and charterer will know that economically it makes sense to fill your tanker rather than transport empty space 'dead freight'[8] around so in the very early days at Sullom Voe they endeavoured to achieve this, but things changed with the arrival of 15-day Brent as described later.

At the time, the two streams were segregated and delivered separately but it did not take the Ninian system long to realise that commingling with the higher value light sweet Brent crude would afford them a higher market price. I recall many animated discussions between the various Field and pipeline system operators, including BP, BNOC, Chevron and Shell. They had to agree price differentials for the various oil fields generally based on modelled refinery netbacks from processing the crude qualities. Following the conclusion of those negotiations, the Brent blend quickly established itself as a North Sea benchmark.[9]

ARRIVAL OF 15-DAY TRADING

So, a full month before the month of loading, a lifting programme for Month M+1 would be agreed, and we could expect 'TBN' nominations to be replaced by named tanker nominations in accordance with the Sullom Voe Terminal Operating Procedures and the Brent and Ninian Pipeline Agreements in which nominating and lifting procedures were mirrored.

Short voyage times of the North Sea oil almost certainly shaped a change in the trading patterns from traditional long-haul and long-term contracts towards spot and forward trading.

This led to the creation of the 15-day Brent contract with an initial nominal cargo size of 500,000 barrels also known as parcel size. The Parcel size of 500 kb applied between 1983 and 1985 and increased to 600 kb thereafter which provided better terminal throughput management and was more compatible with Tanker sizes trading out of the North Sea

With Sullom Voe throughput at some 1.2 million barrels per day it was easy to work out that there could be approximately 60 cargo nominations per month to be physically delivered as per the Operating Agreement.

However, the number of Brent-15 day forward month trading contracts could be many times greater than the number of cargos physically available which ultimately meant that the same cargo could be traded multiple times therefore a method of matching from a matrix of forward trades with physical cargoes was required.

The reason for this was that many existing and new trading houses came to the party attracted by the potential profits to be made by forward trading Brent Blend. In addition to the producers such as BP, BNOC, Chevron,Elf, Conoco, Enterprise, Shell, Texaco, Total et al. we found ourselves engaging with a plethora of traders joining in over the years and by memory these included Arcadia, Cargill, Jaron (Goldman Sachs), Drexel Burnham Lambert, Phibro, Transworld Oil, Gatoil, Petrodiamond, Marc Rich (resurrected as Glencore), Morgan Stanley, Mercuria, Gunvor, Trafigura, Vitol and others.

A notable exception was the world's largest oil company, Exxon, which chose to focus on its core business of producing, refining and marketing.

The 15-day process determined that Seller shall declare to Buyer the Laydays and the Cargo Reference Number in respect of the cargo in the month ahead (month M + 1) not later than (the time shall be of the essence in this respect), 1700 hours London time on the 15th Day prior to the first Day of the Laydays.

At the beginning of the Brent trading, the oil majors attempted to amend their own General Terms and Conditions (GTCs) of sale to reflect these processes, but as always in contract negotiations, there were differences of interpretation, and some disputes arose.

Eventually, all saw sense, and the Shell UK Oil (SUKO) 1990 Agreement for the Sale of Brent Blend Crude Oil on 15-Day Terms[10] was widely adopted by the industry. Under SUKO terms, Brent Blend 15-day trades were delivered 'free on board' (FOB), at Sullom Voe terminal, with a string of FOB sales until an end user chartered a Tanker and took physical delivery into a refinery or sometimes into storage.

PASS THE PARCEL

What all the foregoing led to was something akin to the kid's party game of 'pass the parcel', except that when the music stopped at 1700 hours London time, the player with the parcel may have an unwanted gift.

The original owner of each cargo in the lifting programme established for each month needed to decide not later than 15 days prior to the date of the lifting whether to retain the physical cargo and arrange for its lifting by tanker in the contractual date range (Laydays) or declare it as a 15-day or a forward Brent cargo.

In the latter case, Pursuant to Section 3 Laydays of the SUKO 1990 terms,[11] the Seller was obliged to make a telephone declaration to one of its Buyers not later than 1700 hours London time on the 15th day prior to the first day of the Laydays specifying the parcel number, date and contract price. i.e., for a declaration made on the first Day of the Specified Month, the earliest Laydays acceptable was 16th–18th of the Specified Month.

Telephone declarations made by 1700 hours were considered valid but had to be promptly confirmed by telex from Seller.

If the 15th Day prior to the first Day of the Laydays was a Saturday, Sunday or London Bank Holiday then such declaration was to be made not later than 1700 hours on the last preceding London Banking Day.

It quickly became evident that advance knowledge of the details of the finally agreed loading programme could give a competitive edge therefore the Brent System Coordinator did not publish the programme until midnight on the 16th day prior to the first day of the Loading Month.

Each Buyer receiving a declaration was obliged to either keep the cargo or declare it to one of its own Buyers under the same process.

In most cases, the cargo would be passed on so that gradually from a matrix of forward month deals a trade chain would develop. Operators would continuously track the 'daisy chain' and converse with counterparts to try and determine who would be passing to who, but this was very much a hit and miss exercise.[12] As 1700 hours London time approached things became tense and quite nerve wracking.

I set up my Geneva team such that one operator stood by the designated incoming phone to receive incoming declarations with two further operators ready to dial out. The operator receiving the oncoming call would repeat out loud the parcel number and date range for the declaration and the outgoing operators would pass these on to the first buyer to pick up.

The Brent traders, notably my old pals Rex Steed and Kurt Chapman,[13] and I would keep away from the oil operations (usually referred to as 'ops') desk, so as not to add more pressure to the tense few minutes just before the deadline time which, in our case, was 1800 Geneva time.

If we were 'clocked'—which meant that there was no time to pass on the declaration, then the first step was to determine with the Brent system coordinator whether the scheduled Lay days could be deferred by one day with the agreement of the equity producer(s) of the cargo. If this was possible the cargo remained a forward Brent cargo and could be declared again the following day. The whole process would run again, until 1700 London time on that day. If this was not achievable, traders would not be happy and whilst not blaming my ops team, would skulk around the trading room with very glum faces as the cargo could be considered distressed.

If a company ended up with a 'clocked' cargo, then they would have the responsibility of ensuring that a vessel was chartered and arrived on time, to take delivery of the cargo within the declared Laydays. The 15-day cargo with declared dates and a cargo number thus became a 'Dated' Brent cargo, ready for a physical delivery. If nobody wanted to keep the declared cargo, chances were that the market was weak and that the Dated Brent cargo was worth less than a 15-day (forward Brent) cargo, loading in the same month.

This was not a good position to be in as the entire market would be aware that there was a 'distressed' cargo looking for a home. Not a commercially good position to be in—the acquired Dated Brent cargo through 'clocking' would be worth less than the purchased 15-day Brent and the company was certain to make a loss. If Dated Brent was trading a dollar below the forward (15-day Brent), the company would lose half a million dollars[14] just through a bad fortune of not being able to pass on the nominated cargo.

Despite the requirement to pass them on as expeditiously some companies would sit on dates in an effort to thwart the system to their advantage often trying to use the excuse of different time zones as an excuse. This was not always a wise practice as they could soon find themselves targeted for 'clocking' by other players. Transworld Oil (TWO) were often suspected of delaying the passing on of dates using the excuse of time difference with their Bermuda operations team. My operations (ops) team, and others would call the TWO operator to try and put pressure on to disclose to whom they would pass the dates. This was not always successful and led to some heated exchanges, as it happened.

In the case of companies with their own refining systems this was not such major problem, however, logistically unhelpful but for trading companies with no system could be expensive.[15]

Eventually, all of the nominated cargoes for the month would need to be physically loaded. In many cases, during the declaration period, traders and operators would work together and converse with their counterparts in other companies to try to match buys and sells to construct chains such that two or more profit making trades were placed in the same chain.[16] This was a haphazard process which could also be used to place loss making trades in a chain.

If a company was successful in placing two or more trades in a single chain and then take physical delivery, they could nominate to load either the plus 5 per cent loading tolerance or the minus 5 per cent loading tolerance, in order to maximise profit or minimise loss. Strictly speaking, the loading tolerance was supposed to be a shipping tolerance compatible with the tanker carrying capacity but was regularly used for purely financial reasons.

Between 1983 and 1985, the 500 thousand barrel (kb) cargo nomination would contain instructions to load 'as close to but no less than 475,000 barrels' or 'as close as possible but not exceeding 525,000 barrels'. After 1985, this became not less than 570 kb and not exceeding 630 kb.[17]

Most cargoes were physically lifted as a single parcel on LR1 tankers. However, there was nothing to prevent a company loading up to 4 nominal cargoes on a VLCC, although this was rare.

Equity producers could also sell small 'top up' parcels to help make maximum use of ship's cargo space.

FAILED PHYSICAL MARKET SQUEEZE

As the 15-day market matured, some traders attempted to squeeze the market by keeping as many physical dates as possible, but this often led to their downfall.

One such company was TWO (mentioned earlier for not playing the pass the parcel game fairly) were headed up by the infamous Dutch Trader John Deuss. In 1988, Deuss bought up almost all the Brent crude cargoes for an alleged $425 million. He expected oil prices to rise, since he controlled the available supply. The story went that Shell and Exxon had secretly teamed up to organise additional Brent cargoes.[18] When Shell leaked their plan to the media, Deuss realised he had been outmanoeuvred and was forced to sell the shipments at a loss of $600 million.

As an aside, I once visited John Deuss's mansion in the Netherlands and underwent a search by armed bodyguards at the entrance gate and again at the building entry, a somewhat daunting experience.

Book Outs

In the 1980s and 1990s, trading chains established for each Brent cargo could be in excess of 100 trades. This would mean that each buyer in turn would need to pass loading and documentary instructions through the trade chain to the loading terminal, and after loading, each seller in turn would be contractually obliged to pass original bills of lading and other cargo documents to its original buyer.

This was quickly seen to be a cumbersome administrative process as, apart from the original equity producer, charterer, shipowner and end receiver no one else in the chain had much interest in the physical cargo.

Often the same company names would appear twice or more in the trade chains established for each cargo. In order to ease the administrative burden a process was developed whereby large sections of the chain could be circumvented by a 'book out'. A book out is closing of an open position of a contract between two or more parties, before it matures (before oil becomes physical). This entails a company appearing twice in a chain, obtaining agreement for all the companies in between its own positions to agree to settle their contractual obligations by setting a base price for cash settlement. This could remove large section of the physical chain, making the eventual physical nominations easier.

For example, take the following chain:

BP-*ETSA*-Phibro-Aron-Arcadia-TWO-*ETSA*-Shell-Refinery

ETSA would seek to obtain agreement from Phibro, Aron, Arcadia and TWO to cancel the sales between the two ETSA positions basis an agreed base price with cash settlement of the differences between the contract prices and the base price applied to the nominal cargo size. ETSA would then take delivery from BP and deliver to Shell removing Phibro, Aron, Arcadia and TWO from any further obligations.

PAYMENT TERMS

Payment terms under Suko 1990 GT&Cs were 30 days after completion of loading, upon presentation of Invoice, 3 original bills of lading and supporting shipping documents (typically Certificates of Quantity, Quality, Origin and Time sheet).

If the documents were not available when payment was due, then the Seller would issue a letter of Indemnity (LOI) to the Buyer for missing documents. More on LOIs in the section 'Paper Chase and Letters of Indemnity' below.

Major players such as BP, Shell, Elf, Total would trade on open credit without requiring payment security[19] whereas most of the other players would be required to provide payment security usually in the form of a 'documentary letter of credit' from a bank, acceptable to the Seller. Bank charges would be for buyers account and could be quite significant, dependent on the bank's assessment of the company's credit and the risk involved.

On occasion when the oil trading company was a subsidiary of a larger corporation such as PetroDiamond who were owned by Mitsubishi, a 'parent company guarantee' was accepted by the seller.

However, this could be a problem. I recall my credit department accepting a parent Company Guarantee for Drexel Burnham Oil Trading from its parent Drexel Burnham Lambert (an American multinational investment bank) that was forced into bankruptcy in 1990, due to its involvement in illegal activities in the junk bond market. The news broke when we had open purchase and sale positions with them, and I worked late into the night with other exposed companies to construct a trade chain enabling us to arrange a book out which removed Drexel Burnham Oil Trading from the chain, thereby avoiding the chain collapsing and legal actions which would have dragged on for years.

Physical Volumes at Sullom Voe started to decline in April 2002 led to a reduction of the numbers of physical cargos available at Sullom Voe. Also, Shell UK reduced the operational tolerance (in their SUKO 1990 GT&Cs) from 5 per cent to 1 per cent. To counter this trend and increase liquidity in the Brent contract, Platts introduced other North Sea Crudes such as Forties, loading at Hound Point terminal, Scotland, Norwegian Oseberg loading at Sture terminal and Ekofisk, produced in Norway, but loading at the UK Teesside terminal. However, these changes did not lead to increased forward Brent activity, at least from the operations point of view.

Paper Chase and Letters of Indemnity

During the peak years, even after book outs long trade chains remained through which Bills of lading would need to pass from each Seller to each Buyer.

The bill of lading (B/L) serves as both a receipt for goods to be transported and as evidence of Title to the goods historically three original bills of lading are produced and signed by the Master at the loading terminal.

Oil tankers loading physical cargoes are contracted under an agreement between the shipowner and the charterer, known as a Charter Party (CP). CP stipulates that an original bill of lading must be produced to the master of the vessel[20] at the destination port in order to discharge the cargo.

The sales contracts for the Brent blend stipulate[21] that the seller must present all three original bills of lading together with the Invoice in order to receive the payment for the cargo.

Clearly, the B/L document cannot be in two places at once. To add to this complication, the B/Ls need to be manually endorsed from each seller to each buyer, along the entire trade chain.

This was not physically possible to achieve prior to discharge or even the payment due date, so the industry bypassed the requirement by issuing Letters of Indemnity (LOIs),[22] one between the tanker charterer to the tanker owner to enable the discharge of the cargo and another from each seller to each buyer to obtain payment.

Many hours were wasted discussing LOI wording, until eventually two or three standard formats were agreed that most players used. Basically, the LOIs were all designed to achieve the same workaround when documents were not available. But pride of authorship and conflicting legal opinions got in the way until eventually, the wording of the LOI in the appendix C of the SUKO 1990 GT&Cs was accepted by a majority of Brent players.

However, there were few exceptions—a notable one was BP who still liked to use their own wording, not too dissimilar from Shell's LOI wording. My personal opinion was that there was little difference and at ETSA we took a pragmatic approach using either the SUKO or BP wording.

Where the sale was financially secured by a letter of credit, it was frequently a requirement that an LOI should be countersigned by the seller's (bank at an additional cost to the seller).

Due to the logistics of mailing or couriering the original paper B/Ls through several global office locations, they moved very slowly through the trading chain. As an authorised signatory for ETSA, I recall signing an endorsement on one B/L more than a year after the vessel had loaded and discharged. Upon closer inspection of the document, I found my signature on two earlier endorsements of the same document, where ETSA appeared more than twice in the trading chain.

In practice, the B/L was never available at the discharge port, and it was rarely produced at the end of a trade chain. Therefore, LOIs were the rule rather than the exception. In theory these documents should count as a contingent liability on the issuer's Balance sheet, but few players took this into account. Some companies, in particular banks, spent a lot of time trying to track down missing documents. Sometimes the documents never showed up and were just left forgotten in some office cupboard, leaving the LOI outstanding for years—but few cared.

In reality these LOIs did not guarantee payment but were a basis for the commencement of a claim against the defaulting party. This led to long and costly legal actions which we often settled out of court.

Because of the obvious breakdown of the paper B/L processes, I became an early advocate for electronic bills of lading. But even now, in 2023, this idea is only just beginning to gain traction. In Jan 2023, the Intercontinental Exchange (ICE) launched its Dated, digital trade document service, which may provide some impetus.

15 Years of Operating Brent

During the years of peak activity of the forward Brent trading (approximately between 1985 and 1999), many of the operations people got to know each other well and many long-lasting friendships developed.

In February each year, the Institute of Petroleum organises its annual dinner, which became the trigger for hundreds of oil traders and operators to descend on London for a week of networking and deal making. This was an excuse for several of the players to throw extravagant parties. BP organised an event for operations folk only—an event for which invites were keenly sought. Trading houses Phibro and Vitol would vie to give the most extravagant parties in Park Lane and Mayfair hotels, often hiring popular music performers of the time such as Bucks Fizz. The Institute's formal annual dinner is still held every year, but the party scene diminished as companies realised that it was not only expensive but, but started to generate a negative public image.

After a career spanning over 40 years in oil supply, trading and shipping I recall the 15 years I spent managing the Brent operations as the most exciting and, at the same time, frustrating time.

It was exciting as the traditional supply and trading world was completely shaken up, leading to innovative ways of doing things. Sometimes, it was frustrating because of the devious behaviour of some of the players and their large egos. Above all, I came out of this period with very fond memories of great camaraderie amongst my fellow operations colleagues.

NOTES

1. Terms were generally borrowed from financial and other commodity markets.
2. Market structure in which prompt delivery is trading at a premium to forward delivery.
3. Opposite of backwardation. Structure in which the forward prices trade at a premium to prompt delivery.
4. Partials are small volumes or 'parts' of whole cargoes. Top-ups are same, but with a specific intent to fill up the vessel and thus minimise per barrel freight.
5. Liz Bosley and Colin Bryce also worked at BNOC.
6. https://fr.wikipedia.org/wiki/Bernard_de_Combret.
7. 'At its peak in the 1980s, the terminal was processing over 1.5 million barrels of oil a day and by 1997 the six billionth barrel of crude oil was produced at the terminal, highlighting the importance the facility had to the UK economy'. https://www.shetnews.co.uk/2018/11/23/forty-years-and-counting-for-oil-at-sullom-voe/.
8. Fixed freight divided by more barrels equals less cost of shipping per each barrel.
9. Trading colleagues contributing to this book will expand on these terms.
10. See https://www.shell.com/business-customers/trading-and-supply/trading/general-trading-terms-and-conditions.html.
11. https://www.shell.com/business-customers/trading-and-supply/trading/general-trading-terms-and-conditions/_jcr_content/root/main/section/simple/call_to_action/links/item0.stream/1660220692851/b931d33c747087213e9b32577e36e978b1fd1668/suko90-fob-brent15-day1990gtcs.pdf.

12. The operators were not obliged to give this information and the quality of information mainly depended on good relationships between the operators.
13. Kurt Chapman is also an author of a chapter in this book.
14. For a cargo of 500,000, barrels, which was trading in the 1990s, times $1 a barrel equals $500,000.
15. Integrated companies with own refining systems could usually place the cargo in their own refinery (albeit at a loss).
16. For details of the 'profitable' chains due to optimisation of tolerance, see the chapter by Kurt Chapman.
17. SUKO 1990 GT&Cs gave the buyer (or end user) the option to choose the volume loaded within the 5 per cent tolerance. Later, it was reduced to 1 per cent.
18. This can be done by moving cargoes from previous $(M-1)$ or nect $(M+1)$ month of loading, subject to production availability.
19. Payment security could take a form of a bank guarantee (usually in the form of a 'letter of credit') or a parent company guarantee.
20. Captain of the vessel.
21. SUKO GT&C 1990 Section 5—payment and Appendix C.
22. Essentially, LOI promises delivery of the said documents at a later stage.

REFERENCES

SUKO (Shell UK Oil) 1990 Agreement for the Sale of Brent Blend Crude Oil on 15-Day Terms.

Sullom Voe Terminal Operating Agreement between Shell UK Ltd and BP Petroleum Development, 19 March 1979. (Upon the demise of BNOC I kept Confirmed Copy N0 158 as a keepsake).

CHAPTER 7

Brent and the International Petroleum Exchange

David Peniket

Abstract This chapter is a fascinating story of how a small, electronic platform eventually bought a major oil exchange. Electronic trading had solid support from some of the biggest names and liquidity providers in oil trading: BP, Shell, Total, Goldman Sachs, and Morgan Stanley. In return, investing in the exchange was probably the most profitable venture they ever made. It is also a story of how the selfish interest of a few entrenched incumbents, supporting the old, open outcry trading method can backfire spectacularly.

Keywords Electronic trading · ICE · Liquidity · Open outcry

D. Peniket (✉)
Berkhamsted, UK
e-mail: davidjpeniket@gmail.com

A. Imsirovic (ed.), *Brent Crude Oil*,
https://doi.org/10.1007/978-3-031-28232-4_7

When I joined the International Petroleum Exchange of London Limited (IPE) as Head of Finance in January 1999, the Exchange's Brent Futures contract had been trading for over a decade and was already a success. Brent Futures and Options traded a daily average of over 60,000 contracts that month—the equivalent of 60 million barrels of notional crude oil—84% of daily global crude oil production. Brent accounted for 70% of IPE volume.[1] As the market moved from open outcry to electronic trading, and the Brent complex continued to grow in importance, that success was to continue. By January 2023 Brent was to trade a daily average of over 1.1 million contracts—the equivalent of 12 times daily global production—an 18-fold increase on twenty-four years earlier.

ESTABLISHMENT OF THE IPE

The IPE was founded in 1980 and began trading its first contract (IPE Gas Oil Futures) in April 1981.[2] Much of the initial work to establish the IPE was done by the London Commodity Exchange (LCE), which provided a market for trading in soft commodities such as coffee, cocoa, and rubber. Following the launch of the New York Mercantile Exchange's (NYMEX) Heating Oil futures contract, the LCE saw an opportunity to create a similar venue in London. Keen to encourage oil industry participation, the LCE persuaded the 30-year-old Robin Woodhead (who worked for Premier Oil[3]) to become the IPE's first Chairman. It was at the LCE's premises on Mark Lane in the City of London where the very first trading on the IPE took place.

Like other similar exchanges, the development of the IPE was financed by the sale of 'seats' which brought with them the right to trade on the market. Seats on the IPE were sold to London commodity brokers who saw the opportunity to participate in the growth of the oil market, and the Exchange raised an initial £700,000 from floor members.[4] In May 1987, the Exchange added a number of 'local' seats which were made available to individuals trading on their own account.[5]

A commodity futures contract is defined by the US Commodity Futures Trading Commission (CFTC) as an agreement to buy or sell a particular commodity at a future date.[6] The price and the amount of the commodity are fixed at the time of the agreement. Although many such futures contracts can lead to physical delivery, it is perfectly possible to trade in and out of a futures contract without ever actually making or taking delivery of the underlying commodity. This feature opens up futures markets to a much broader group of participants than those with access to the physical market. Exchanges typically offer a number of contracts with different future expiry dates—often at monthly intervals for nearer dates and six-monthly or annual intervals for those further ahead. This range of expiry dates allows the development of a 'forward curve' which helps participants in the market to understand the price relationships between different time periods. Futures trading also adds central clearing—which was provided at the outset of the IPE by the International Commodities Clearing House, the forerunner of the London Clearing House (LCH) (today part of the London Stock Exchange Group). A Clearing House guarantees the performance of every trade—becoming the buyer to every seller, and the seller to every buyer. This protects market participants from losses if their counterparty defaults.

For its first 25 years, trading on the IPE, as with most other commodity futures markets, took place by 'open outcry,' where traders would shout bids and offers across a trading floor. At Mark Lane, this happened in trading rings, but after the Exchange's move to Commodity Quay in May 1987, trading took place in tiered pits[7] surrounded by banks of phones. Hand signals started to be used by the traders to help confirm what was being shouted as the pits became noisier. Clerks would take orders from clients which were then quickly communicated into the pit. Exchange staff at the pit's centre would listen to the bids and offers and maintain a running commentary of quoted bids, offers, and trades. Other staff would key this information into a price feed—which was conveyed both to wallboards above the pit and to quote vendors such as Reuters and Bloomberg who would stream prices to screens around the world.

LAUNCH OF BRENT FUTURES

From the outset of the IPE, crude oil futures were seen as part of the longer-term plan.[8] In November 1983 the IPE launched the first iteration of its Brent Futures contract, originally designed to be delivered inter-tank (physical) or in-tank (by book transfer between the seller and buyer) in the Amsterdam-Rotterdam-Antwerp (ARA) area.[9] In March 1983, NYMEX had launched their West Texas Intermediate (WTI) Futures contract[10] which was based on pipeline delivery in Cushing Oklahoma. The problem for those designing a North Sea alternative was that crude oil was available for loading at Sullom Voe only to those able to handle parcels of 500,000 barrels, the equivalent of 500 lots of futures.[11] Sally Clubley, who worked for Premier Man, a broker, recalls: '*The first one that was in-tank Rotterdam...that isn't a market. Nobody knew what Brent in-tank in Rotterdam was worth. At that stage everyone felt there had to be a physical delivery that was possible. And obviously you couldn't have a minimum delivery size of 500,000 barrels – that wasn't going to work. You had to be able to take delivery of a small quantity. That was the only solution people could find.*'[12] As well as the lack of an underlying physical market, the access to storage was relatively restricted. Participants risked being caught with positions running into expiry which could give rise to obligations to make or take delivery that they might not be able to fulfil.[13]

The solution the Exchange devised to the physical delivery problem was the creation of the IPE Brent Index, against which all open positions on expiry of Brent Futures were settled. The Brent Index was based on trades in and assessments of the North Sea forward market.[14] Allowing positions to default to financial settlement removed the risk that participants would inadvertently be forced into delivery. Settlement of this kind is common in financial derivatives (such as interest rate or equity index futures like those based on the FTSE 100 or S&P 500). However, this was relatively rare for commodity futures markets, and represented a departure from the traditional definition of a commodity futures contract.[15]

In October 1985, the Exchange launched its first financially settled Brent contract which expired against an index of trades over a five day window, but liquidity still failed to grow.[16] Then, in 1988, the Index was modified to be based only on forward market trades on futures expiry day, and the contract's expiry was brought forward from the fifteenth to the tenth trading day of the month.[17] The contract was re-launched on 23 June 1988[18] and was supported by an incentive scheme involving the issue of new trading permits to existing members and their sale to new participants. The change in Index specification created a more easily tradeable link with the already liquid Brent forward market, and the new mechanism served to unlock a barrier to participation for many traders.

Two other factors provided the foundation for the subsequent growth of Brent futures. First, the Brent partials market developed, which allowed trading in the North Sea forward market with contracts of 50,000 barrels—the equivalent of 50 lots of futures.[19] Second, the revised contract came to the market at a time when Middle Eastern producers were moving away from OPEC's administration of the oil price. The new system was market-based—the pricing was based on a formula where a particular crude's price was related back to movements in the price of a more general benchmark.[20] The Brent complex rapidly became established as the benchmark for Europe, and, over time, for most of the world outside the US.

Trading activity in IPE Brent grew rapidly, with over 500,000 contracts traded in 1988, putting volumes on a par with Gas Oil Futures by early 1989. Traded options on Brent futures were introduced in May 1989 and Iraq's invasion of Kuwait in August 1990 and the subsequent Gulf War further accelerated the growth of the contract. Political events in the Middle East tended to happen overnight, and the IPE floor during the London morning was perfectly positioned to react before NYMEX opened at 3:00 p.m. London time.[21]

At the same time, volumes on the NYMEX WTI contract grew, and both markets benefited from arbitrage between the two. At first the markets were clearly complementary rather than competitive—although the rise of electronic trading was to mean that each market would become a threat to the other.

DEMUTUALISATION

'*In five years' time, all exchanges will be electronic, and they will all have demutualised,*' Lynton Jones told me during my interview for the position of Head of Finance at the IPE in the autumn of 1998. I had spent seven years at KPMG where I qualified as an accountant, and I was now looking for a move into a line role. It was pretty clear from my interview that things might be turbulent, but energy markets were liberalising, the pace of technological change was accelerating, and the growth of Brent meant that the business was profitable—it was an exciting opportunity.

In August 1996 Jones had succeeded Peter Wildblood as Chief Executive of the IPE. Following a career in the Foreign Office, he worked at the London Stock Exchange and Nasdaq before running the OM London Exchange (OMLX). Jones could see that electronic trading had huge potential to disrupt futures markets and believed that the IPE should expand its own electronic offering. Before Jones had joined, the IPE's Chief Technology Officer Mike O'Donnell had already begun work on the Exchange's own electronic trading system—ETS—which was used for the launch of the IPE's UK Natural Gas Futures contract in January 1997.[22]

At this time, NYMEX became increasingly interested in working more closely with the IPE. The two exchanges cooperated on electronic trading platform development, and informal talks led to more serious discussions. In November 1997, NYMEX Chairman Danny Rappaport endorsed a possible merger with the IPE. 'I think it's a unique strategic opportunity to ensure the continued strength of the global futures market,' he said.[23] But by the autumn of 1998 Jones become clear in his own mind that acquisition by NYMEX was not the best path for the IPE, and he started to explore alternatives.[24] He felt that the mutual ownership structure of both the IPE and NYMEX was wrong—both exchanges were owned by those with a vested interest in the continuity of open outcry, to whom electronic trading was a serious threat. If this structure was not changed, he felt that new competitors would emerge. Two years previously, London's LIFFE market had seen its share of futures on the German long-term government bond, the Bund, start to erode. Volumes shifted from the LIFFE open outcry pits to the electronic trading screens of Frankfurt's DTB. LIFFE's share of Bund volume had been 70% in July 1996 but by October 1998 all of the volume in the contract had moved to the DTB.[25] LIFFE was forced to accelerate the development of its own electronic platform and to close its open outcry pits as it battled to survive. The lesson was clear: the transition to electronic trading was inevitable and exchanges needed to adapt quickly or risk a repeat of what had happened with the Bund.

When I joined the IPE, I had assumed that I would have some time to get to understand the Exchange's business before any potential merger or acquisition activity was to take place. However, within a few weeks, I was called into Jones's office for a meeting with him and Richard Ward, the Director of Business Development. Jones explained that he felt the IPE needed an alternative to a deal with NYMEX. He and Ward believed that the IPE needed new outside investors who would be committed to a transition to electronic trading. They wanted me to start work on a valuation of the business to help them and Head of Legal Dee Blake to put a plan together.

Jones had met Enron President Jeff Skilling at an event in New York hosted by NYMEX and secured a meeting with him on the sidelines of an Enron event in London.

Jones explained to Skilling that he felt that a deal with NYMEX was not going to happen. '*I was thinking that we ought to try and take this thing independent – commercial - would he be interested in becoming an owner? And he asked me a few questions. He said "OK, we'll do it."*' Jones and Ward also secured interest from other investors, putting together a proposal they called 'Plan B' whereby Enron, OM, Nord Pool, Distrigas, and British Gas would together invest £25 million in return for 70% of the Exchange's equity.

NYMEX's interest remained, and they made a low offer for the IPE which they later increased to £19.6 million for 55% of the Exchange, in an attempt to match Plan B.[26] NYMEX CEO Danny Rappaport travelled to London and met with the IPE Board to seek its support, but they were unimpressed.

On the 7 July, the IPE Board voted to endorse the Plan B proposal, which included a pledge to maintain open outcry trading until at least September 2001. The Exchange was seeking to achieve both demutualisation (the separation of ownership rights from trading rights) and a change of ownership in a single step. Jones set about winning support from the trading firms and local members who owned the Exchange.

Mark Cutter, the local representative on the IPE Board and his predecessor Jon Maidman had secured agreement that each local seat would be worth 25% of a full seat, so local seat holders stood to share the payout from the proposed sale. Many agreed to support the proposal while hoping to ensure that the life of the floor would be extended for as long as possible. But the transaction was opposed by other locals and a number of floor brokers, in particular the largest broker Man Group plc (later MF Global). Man CEO Kevin Davis had built the largest clearing business in London, and did not want the IPE's open outcry model to change. And he felt the IPE was being sold too cheaply.[27] NYMEX wrote to IPE members urging them to reject the proposal.

On 30 July 1999, the IPE Chairman Lord Fraser chaired an Extraordinary General Meeting of the Exchange where the result of the vote was announced. The proposal had secured 63.71% of the votes—not enough to achieve the 75% majority required.[28] Jones and Lord Fraser resigned that day, leaving the Exchange in the hands of Deputy Chairman Colin Bryce of Morgan Stanley, and of Richard Ward, who became Acting CEO. Those of us who had worked on Plan B were very disappointed: the plan had not been perfect but had set a clear direction of travel. Our CEO had gone and those who were opposed to electronic trading had a blocking minority that they might use again.

Bryce was called into the UK Regulator, the Financial Services Authority, by Gay Huey Evans, who headed the FSA's Markets Division.[29] The FSA were concerned that instability at the IPE could have an impact on market confidence and the reputation of the City. They wanted to identify a senior figure capable of taking the helm as Chair of the Exchange. Colin Bryce recognised the need for someone to stabilise the operation, but also wanted to find a person who understood the oil industry and would have the vision to help the IPE to achieve its potential.

Sir Bob Reid, who had led Shell UK and later chaired British Rail, was identified as the best candidate. Bryce recalls: '*I'd never met him but knew of him as a head of Shell UK and had read about him – a fellow Scot. So, I thought, well here's a person who's senior, very clearly highly respected, and would know the business.*'

Sir Bob became Chairman on 12 August 1999[30] and took time to meet with the Board and the Exchange's members. He decided to break down the process of demutualisation into two phases, first changing the ownership structure to separate ownership and trading rights and only then to consider how bring in external investment. The demutualisation proposals were approved by an overwhelming majority of members in February 2000. An important milestone had been reached.

Enron Online

Enron's interest in electronic trading pre-dated their involvement with Plan B. In June 1996 John Sherriff, who later became President and CEO of Enron Europe, had proposed in an internal study that Enron should experiment with a one-to-many electronic trading platform.[31] In April 1999 Sherriff and his boss Greg Whalley charged Louise Kitchen, Head of Enron's European Gas and Power trading business, with the development of a global online trading system.

After an intense six-month project, Kitchen was ready to unveil EnronOnline. Ahead of a public announcement on 26 October, Kitchen and her colleagues invited major oil market participants including Morgan Stanley to a presentation in Monte Carlo on 15 and 16 September to encourage them to take part. The meeting made a deep impression on Colin Bryce, though not in the way that Enron might have hoped:

'They gave us this whole spiel and I thought, hang on a minute here, we are the liquidity providers,' he recalls. *'Where's the value? The value is in liquidity. These guys are going to set this thing up - Enron to the world, the world to Enron - using our value and our liquidity.'*[32]

Bryce flew to New York to talk to his boss Neal Shear. He knew that Morgan Stanley would need to work with Goldman Sachs if they were to create something with any chance of rivalling EnronOnline and sought and obtained legal clearance to talk to them. He invited Isabelle Ealet and Dick Bronks of Goldman Sachs to breakfast with him and his colleague Goran Trapp at Morgan Stanley's offices at 25 Cabot Square on 15 December. Bryce and Trapp outlined their plan: they needed to assemble liquidity providers, get a system built, and set up an electronic market for OTC products.

'*To our complete surprise Dick and Isabelle were completely on board with that. So they went away and by two or three o'clock in the afternoon, I got a call from Dick, "We are with you on it, Gary Cohn has approved it."*' Cohn, who went on to become President of Goldman Sachs, was then running the firm's global commodity business. He was also a member of the NYMEX Board. Goldman assigned Partner Tim O'Neill[33] to lead the project on their side and Morgan Stanley assigned Harold Kamins, who was their head of options.

The firms needed a trading platform and discussed whether they should build one themselves. As the dot-com boom was peaking at the time, there were several start-up trading platforms looking for the backing of liquidity providers, so they also explored whether there was a platform they could acquire. They looked at several alternatives including Altra (jointly owned by the brokers Prebon and Amerex), Houston Street and a platform called CPEX owned by an entrepreneur called Jeffrey Sprecher.

INTERCONTINENTAL EXCHANGE

Sprecher was an engineer with a background in the US power industry. With the growth of the internet, he saw that there was a big opportunity to bring transparent electronic trading to the US gas and power markets. Having spent some time in Europe studying how the Nord Pool[34] market operated, Sprecher bought a small trading platform called CPEX (originally part of the Berkshire Hathaway subsidiary MidAmerican Energy). He let most of the staff go but retained Chuck Vice, who became Sprecher's partner in building the business, and Edwin Marcial, who became the firm's Chief Technology Officer. Sprecher spent months meeting with energy companies, including Enron, and with brokers. In doing so, he was looking to find sources of liquidity for his new platform. In late 1999 he met with energy broker Rafael Pirutinsky who encouraged him to approach Goldman Sachs and Morgan Stanley and helped to secure a meeting with Neal Shear. Sprecher was willing to give away a large proportion of the equity in CPEX in return for trading commitments—exactly the kind of deal that Goldman Sachs and Morgan Stanley were looking for. An agreement with the two investment banks was quickly signed, and Sprecher joined Dick Bronks and Colin Bryce to approach other major traders in the oil markets, including BP, Shell, Société Générale, and Total.

Intercontinental Exchange (ICE) was unveiled in a press release in May 2000.[35] Those of us at the IPE could see that ICE presented us with both risks and opportunities. In BP, Shell, Total, Goldman Sachs, and Morgan Stanley, ICE had five of the major participants in the Brent market. The IPE's own ETS trading platform worked well for the UK natural gas contract, but we thought it was a long way from being capable of supporting the increasing volumes in Brent. We needed a new technology solution and would have to source this from a third party. And we were worried that if ICE and NYMEX were to cooperate, they might pose a serious competitive threat to the IPE. We had been alarmed by reports of a meeting between Jeffrey Sprecher and the NYMEX Board. Sprecher had offered NYMEX a stake in ICE's business in return for agreement to provide clearing services for its OTC gas and power products.[36] Fortunately for the IPE, the NYMEX Board was controlled by open outcry traders who hated the idea of screen trading in any form—Sprecher had been escorted from the building.

Shortly after ICE was announced, Richard Ward called Sprecher to congratulate him, and suggested that they talk about how ICE and the IPE might work together.[37] Sprecher's initial priority was to get access to clearing services. After being rebuffed by NYMEX, he flew to London. He first met with LCH CEO David Hardy and realised that it would be better to work with the IPE, an LCH shareholder, than to try to work around it. The initial meetings went well and both sides quickly saw the opportunities that putting the two businesses together would present. I quickly became convinced that a combination of the two firms could help both ICE and the IPE. ICE had a technology platform and the backing of some of the energy market's major firms; the IPE had experience operating a regulated market and, in the Brent contract, the major international oil benchmark.

Acquisition of the IPE

Richard Ward and Sir Bob travelled to Atlanta and Sprecher made them a proposal. ICE would acquire the IPE for shares which would deliver for its members double the value that had been on the table with Plan B.[38] Half the shares offered (the ICE B shares) would be redeemable for cash, but only once the IPE became fully electronic.[39] Sprecher knew that much of the IPE's trading community might drag their feet and put obstacles in the way of any transition and wanted to ensure that incentives were aligned as far as possible.

In the Offer Document for the IPE, Goldman Sachs set out a large valuation range for Intercontinental Exchange of $400 million to $1.4 billion.[40] This was greeted with scepticism by the IPE's trading community. The dot-com bubble had burst after the NASDAQ Index peaked at 5048 on 10 March 2000[41] and technology valuations had declined significantly; some of the IPE's shareholders felt that the non-redeemable A shares were worth next to nothing. At this stage, however, the trading community could see that we had run out of alternatives. On 18 June 2001, ICE and the IPE announced that shareholders had overwhelmingly approved the acquisition.[42]

However, things were to become more difficult for ICE's US gas and power business. On 2 December 2001, Enron filed for bankruptcy[43] after its aggressive accounting practices unravelled and confidence in the business collapsed. Some of Enron's competitors dramatically scaled back their energy trading operations over the next two years. After an eight-week spike in activity, volumes in ICE's OTC gas and power business declined, and revenues fell significantly.[44]

The Transition to Electronic Trading

Although the acquisition of the IPE was completed in May 2001, and ICE and the IPE were committed to transitioning its business to fully electronic trading, it still took several years before the move was complete. ICE had recruited CME's Product Head David Goone in March 2001 and his initial focus was on delivering OTC clearing facilities to allow its gas and power business to compete with NYMEX's new Clearport offering.[45] Edwin Marcial and ICE's Operations Head Mark Wassersug had work to do on the ICE Platform to adapt it to futures trading and to make it more resilient.

The first step was to introduce out of hours trading for Brent futures on the ICE trading platform so that traders could get used to screen trading at times of day when the pits were not open. Brent screen trading initially operated from 08:00 to 09:45 prior to the opening of the Brent pit. In April 2003 the IPE consulted members on delaying the opening of the Brent pit until 14:00 to allow more time for electronic trading, but there was significant resistance. In response, the Board asked Richard Ward and the management team to explore a strategy based on parallel trading of oil contracts whereby Brent would trade on the screen and in the pit at the same time. But by November it was clear that parallel trading was not going to provide the tipping point required to shift the IPE's business to the screen, and Ward returned to the proposal to delay the opening of the Brent pit until 14:00. The Board approved the proposal to delay the opening by six votes to three.

NYMEX responded quickly. Their President James Newsome announced that they would launch an open outcry trading facility for Brent futures as close as possible to 1 November which was the IPE's planned launch of its fully electronic morning session.[46] The facility would be based at Finex, the Dublin futures operation owned by the New York Board of Trade. NYMEX had a cooperative regulator in the Irish Financial Services Regulatory Authority. Their real objective was to bring a competing open outcry exchange to London, but NYMEX's executives knew that time was of the essence, and that obtaining UK FSA approval for a new Recognised Investment Exchange would take months, if not years. NYMEX offered incentives to London-based traders to relocate to Dublin, including reimbursing living expenses of up to $1000 a week and waiving transaction fees.[47]

The IPE's proposal to reduce the Brent pit hours was not well-received by the market, partly because of scepticism about how far electronic market makers could replace the floor locals. But we pressed ahead, confident that the trading platform was ready.

NYMEX claimed to be encouraged by the initial volumes at their Dublin exchange where trade averaged 5000 lots in the first days after their floor was opened on 1 November. But the extension of the IPE's electronic trading hours went well and an all-time record for electronic Brent of 57,000 contracts was set on 9 November 2004, representing 37% of the total Brent volumes for that day. In January 2005 NYMEX told their Dublin traders that they planned to open a Brent trading floor in London with 1 May as the target date. At a press conference on 14

February Newsome confirmed that it was negotiating a lease for the trading floor and expected to file an application with the FSA within weeks.

When the IPE Board met on Thursday 3 March 2005 Richard Ward told them that the IPE locals accounted for 25–30% of Brent floor volume and a group of customers rumoured to be equity participants in NYMEX's London exchange accounted for another 30%. That meant that 55–60% of the IPE's Brent volume could be at risk. Clearly, the best way to defend the IPE's competitive position was to accelerate the transition to fully electronic trading. Ward was seeking approval for the closure of the floor on 30 days' notice. The Board agreed to consider the proposal over the weekend. When the Board met on the Monday morning, Sir Bob asked each member for their views. Mark Cutter, the locals' representative, said he had friends and colleagues on the floor that he had worked with for many years. He wanted the Exchange to continue to compete both with a trading floor and an electronic platform. But other members spoke in support of the proposal, which was carried by ten votes to one. Sir Bob and Richard Ward went to the trading floor immediately to meet with floor managers who were disappointed but not surprised. Floor closure was scheduled for 7 April.[48]

In the month following floor closure Brent volumes averaged 100,000 lots per day—a very slight fall on the 102,000 lots per day average from January to 7 April. We were relieved that traded volumes had held up: we knew that market participants were getting used to electronic trading, and a number of specialist electronic trading firms were still to increase their activity. But NYMEX continued with its plans to open in London and submitted a Recognised Investment Exchange application to the FSA.

Over the summer, electronic volumes continued to grow. A Brent volume record of 231,000 lots was established on 10 August,[49] up more than 20% on the previous record. Two days later, open interest[50] in IPE Brent exceeded 400,000 lots for the first time. August, normally a quiet month, turned out to be the busiest month for the Exchange on record, with over 4 million lots traded.

NYMEX seemed undeterred and announced that they would start open outcry trading of Brent on their London exchange on 12 September. They traded over 16,000 contracts on the first day and professed optimism that volume and open interest would increase.[51] But volumes dwindled and NYMEX closed their London open outcry operation in June 2006.[52]

The success of the IPE's transition to electronic trading, together with growth in ICE's US OTC gas and power markets, provided ICE with the opportunity to prepare for an Initial Public Offering (IPO). On 26 October 2005 ICE announced that its subsidiaries and business units would operate under the ICE name, and that the IPE would now be known as ICE Futures.[53] On 16 November 2005[54] ICE launched its IPO on the New York Stock Exchange with an offer price of $26, rising 51% on its first day to close at $39.25. This price put the value of ICE at over $2 billion—40% higher than the top end of the valuation range that Goldman Sachs had arrived at four years earlier.

In the years since the transition to electronic trading, Brent volumes have continued to grow. The contract has fundamentally the same form as the version that launched in 1988—financially settled against an index of trades in and assessments of the North Sea forward market on expiry day (Fig. 7.1).

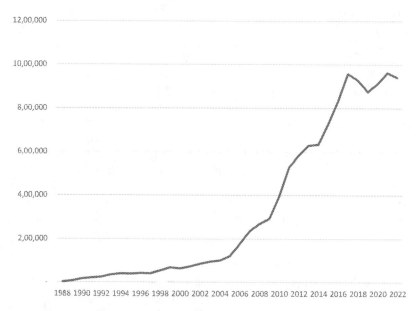

Fig. 7.1 ICE Brent futures—average daily volumes 1988–2022 (*Source* Intercontinental Exchange. Average daily volumes calculated on annual basis)

REGULATED BENCHMARK

Following the LIBOR Scandal, the Financial Conduct Authority announced on 22 December 2014 that it would regulate seven additional UK-based financial benchmarks in the fixed income, commodity, and currency markets from 1 April 2015, and that these would include the ICE Brent Index.[55] Accordingly, ICE Futures Europe was appointed the Benchmark Administrator for the Index. The Exchange established a Brent Index Oversight Committee to oversee the benchmark, chaired by Grahame Cook, a former Crude Oil Trading Manager for BP. In July 2015, ICE confirmed it had a licence for the data used in the Index.[56]

EVOLUTION

As the underlying forward market has evolved,[57] the futures contract has also evolved to reflect changes in that market. More recently, as the need to broaden the complex beyond Brent Blend, Forties Blend, Oseberg, Ekofisk, and Troll crudes became more pressing, ICE and Platts issued a joint white paper and open market consultations on the evolution of the complex.[58] This evolution will involve the inclusion of WTI Midland into the Brent basket of crudes.[59] This will substantially increase the volume of crude oil eligible for the assessment of Brent and potentially, bring the two competing benchmarks much closer together.

NOTES

1. Author's calculations based on volume data from Intercontinental Exchange. See https://www.theice.com/marketdata/reports/7. Daily crude oil production per BP Statistical Review of World Energy. See https://www.bp.com/en/global/corporate/energy-economics/statistical-review-of-world-energy.html.
2. Amos (2021).
3. https://www.harbourenergy.com/about-us/our-history/premier-oil/.
4. International Petroleum Exchange of London Ltd (1982).
5. International Petroleum Exchange of London Ltd (1987).
6. See https://www.cftc.gov/LearnAndProtect/AdvisoriesAndArticles/FuturesMarketBasics/index.htm.
7. International Petroleum Exchange of London Ltd (1987).
8. Author's interview with Robin Woodhead, November 2022.
9. The original contract is described in Horsnell and Mabro (1993, pp. 46–47).

10. See McGrath Goodman (2010, p. 91).
11. Horsnell and Mabro (1993, p. 28).
12. Author's interview with Sally Clubley, December 2022.
13. Horsnell and Mabro (1993, p. 46).
14. The terms 'cash' and 'forward' are used interchangeably here.
15. Technically the ICE Brent Futures is deliverable via Exchange for Physical (EFP) with an option to cash settle. EFPs allow participants to exchange futures positions for equivalent positions in the physical market.
16. Financial Times (1988).
17. Horsnell and Mabro note that this was changed back to the fifteenth day from the July 1990 contract. See Horsnell and Mabro (1993, p. 47).
18. Financial Times (1988)
19. Author's interview with Colin Bryce, October 2022.
20. Horsnell and Mabro (1993, Chapter 15).
21. Nymex brought forward the opening of their pits from 10:00 a.m. to 9:00 a.m. New York time in 2007. See NYMEX (2006).
22. Bossley (1999, p. 33).
23. Reported by Bloomberg News (1997).
24. Author's interview with Lynton Jones, October 2022.
25. The competition between LIFFE and DTB for the Bund contract is summarised in Cantillon and Yin (2007).
26. See Natural Gas Intelligence (1999).
27. Author's interview with Kevin Davis, December 2022.
28. Atkinson (1999).
29. Author's interview with Colin Bryce.
30. Source: Companies House.
31. There is a good account of the development of EnronOnline in Bartlett and Glinska (2001). One-to-many trading platforms are those where all market participants transact with a single market operator. Exchanges like ICE are many-to-many platforms where multitudes of buyers and sellers come together.
32. Author's interview with Colin Bryce.
33. When Tim O'Neill retired from Goldman Sachs in 2022, Sprecher said in an interview 'It's hard to underestimate what a significant role he played in helping us build this company. He's the man behind the curtain. He's the Wizard in The Wizard of Oz.' See Natarajan (2022).
34. https://www.nordpoolgroup.com/en/.
35. Intercontinental Exchange Inc. (2005b, p. 44).
36. Morrison (2008, p. 262).
37. Author's interview with Richard Ward, December 2022.
38. The Offer Document outlined a valuation range for IPE Holdings Plc of £52 million to £92 million. The implied midpoint of £72 million was just over double the £35.7 million valuation from Plan B. See Goldman Sachs International (2001, p. 5).

39. Intercontinental Exchange (2005b, p. 44). In 2004 ICE decided to redeem the B shares early and the redemption payment was made on 23 November 2004.
40. Goldman Sachs International (2001, p. 67).
41. See https://www.cnbc.com/15-years-after-nasdaqs-peak-look-how-its-cha nged/.
42. See Intercontinental Exchange Inc. (2005b, p. 44).
43. Cohn (2021).
44. ICE transaction fees from North American natural gas and power both fell between 2002 and 2003. See Intercontinental Exchange Inc. (2005b, p. 53).
45. Along with Jeffrey Sprecher and Chuck Vice, David Goone was the third key driving force behind the growth of ICE's business.
46. O'Sullivan (2004).
47. Described in NYMEX (2004).
48. Intercontinental Exchange (2005b, p. 47).
49. Ibid.
50. Open interest is the number of contracts or commitments outstanding in futures and options trading on an exchange at any one time.
51. NYMEX (2005).
52. Campbell (2006).
53. Intercontinental Exchange Inc. (2005a). The Exchange then became known as ICE Futures Europe following ICE's 2007 acquisition of the New York Board of Trade which was renamed ICE Futures US.
54. Gelsi (2005).
55. Financial Conduct Authority (2014).
56. Intercontinental Exchange Inc. (2015).
57. For details, see the chapter in this book by Kurt Chapman.
58. S&P Global; Intercontinental Exchange Inc. (2021).
59. More about this will be said in the Epilogue of this book.

BIBLIOGRAPHY

Amos, J.-L. (2021): *Gasoil: Facilitating Transitions to Cleaner Fuels for Forty Years.* https://www.theice.com/insights/market-pulse/energy/gasoil-facilitating-transitions-to-cleaner-fuels-for-forty-years.

Atkinson, D. (1999): 'IPE Chief Quits as Sale Is Voted Down.' *Guardian*, 31 July.

Bartlett, C. A., & Glinska, M. (2001): *EnronOnline: Louise Kitchen, Intrapreneur.* Harvard Business School.

Bloomberg News (1997): 'Nymex Chief Backs Merger With IPE.' *LA Times*, 11 December.

Bossley, L. (1999): *Trading Natural Gas in the UK.* Oxford: Oxford Institute for Energy Studies.

Campbell, A. (2006): 'Nymex Europe to Shut Trading Floor.' *Risk.net*, 6 June.

Cantillon, E., & Yin, P-L. (2007): *How and When Do Markets Tip? Lessons from the Battle of the Bund.* European Central Bank Working Paper Series No. 766, June.

Cohn, S. (2021). *Twenty Years After Epic Bankruptcy, Enron Leaves a Complex Legacy.* https://www.cnbc.com/2021/12/02/twenty-years-after-epic-bankruptcy-enron-leaves-a-complex-legacy.html.

Financial Conduct Authority (2014): *FCA to Regulate Seven Additional Financial Benchmarks.* https://www.fca.org.uk/news/press-releases/fca-regulate-seven-additional-financial-benchmarks.

Financial Times (1988): *IPE to Launch Oil Futures Contract*, June.

Gelsi, S. (2005): 'IntercontinentalExchange IPO Rockets.' *MarketWatch.*

Goldman Sachs International (2001): *Recommended Offer by Goldman Sachs International on Behalf of Intercontinental Exchange, Inc. for IPE Holdings Plc.*

McGrath Goodman, L. (2010): *The Asylum: The Renegades who hijacked the world's oil market.* New York: William Morrow.

Horsnell, P., & Mabro, R. (1993): *Oil Markets and Prices: The Brent Market and the Formation of World Oil Prices.* Oxford: Oxford University Press.

Intercontinental Exchange (2005a): *ICE Futures Europe Circular 05/118: IPE Name Change. ICE Futures Europe Circulars.*

Intercontinental Exchange, Inc. (2005b): *Prospectus Dated November 15, 2005.* New York, NY, United States of America.

Intercontinental Exchange (2015): *ICE Futures Europe Establishes ICE Brent Index Oversight Committee; Licenses ICIS BFOE Market Data.* https://ir.theice.com/press/news-details/2015/ICE-Futures-Europe-Establishes-ICE-Brent-Index-Oversight-Committee-Licenses-ICIS-BFOE-Market-Data/default.aspx.

International Petroleum Exchange of London Limited (1982): *Annual Report for the Period to 31 March 1982.* London.

International Petroleum Exchange of London Limited (1987): *Directors Report and Financial Statements for the Year Ended 31 March 1987.* London.

Morrison, K. (2008): *Living in a Material World: The Commodity Connection.* Chichester: John Wiley & Sons Ltd.

Natarajan, S. (2022): 'Goldman's Celebrated Club Shrinks Further with Tim O'Neill Exit.' *Bloomberg,* 14 December. https://www.bloomberg.com/news/articles/2022-12-14/goldman-s-celebrated-club-shrinks-further-with-tim-o-neill-exit.

Natural Gas Intelligence (1999): IPE Board Turn Its Back on NYMEX. *Natural Gas Intelligence,* 9 July. https://www.naturalgasintel.com/ipe-board-turn-its-back-on-nymex/

NYMEX (2004): *CFTC—NYMEX Submission 04.147: New Temporary NYMEX Incentive Program in Support of the Listing for Trading of the NYMEX Brent Crude Oil Futures Contract on New Dublin Trading Floor,* 28 October. New York, NY, USA.

NYMEX (2005): *NYMEX Europe Pleased with Volume on First Day of Open Outcry Trading in London,* September 12. https://www.cmegroup.com/media-room/press-releases/2005/9/12/_nymex_europe_pleasedwithvolumeonfirstdayofopenoutcrytradinginlo.html.

NYMEX (2006): *NYMEX to Expand Floor Trading Hours for Energy Contracts,* 14 December. https://www.cmegroup.com/media-room/press-releases/2006/12/14/nymex_to_expand_floortradinghoursforenergycontracts.html.

O'Sullivan, J. (2004). 'NYMEX to Open Oil Trading in Dublin.' *Irish Times,* 20 October.

S&P Global; Intercontinental Exchange (2021): *S&P Global Platts and ICE Issue Joint Paper and Open Market Consultations on the Evolution of the Brent Complex,* 21 July. press.spglobal.com. https://press.spglobal.com/2021-07-21-S-P-Global-Platts-and-ICE-Issue-Joint-Paper-and-Open-Market-Consultations-on-the-Evolution-of-the-Brent-Complex.

CHAPTER 8

Brent and the Price Reporting Agencies

Adrian Binks and Neil Fleming

Abstract This chapter is a story of the pivotal role that the PRAs have played in the price discovery for crude oil and therefore oil trading. It explains how the price assessment process evolved together with the changing market. By 'holding up a mirror to the market, in their unique independent and competitive position as benchmark providers, PRAs can also usher in change.'

Keywords PRAs · Price discovery · Platts · Argus

"Price Reporting Agencies" (PRAs)—businesses that report news, write analysis, and publish prices used by commodities markets in term contracts and financial derivatives—have a long historical relationship with

A. Binks (✉) · N. Fleming (✉)
Argus Media Limited, London, England
e-mail: adrian.binks@argusmedia.com

N. Fleming
e-mail: neil.fleming@argusmedia.com

© The Author(s), under exclusive license to Springer Nature Switzerland AG 2023
A. Imsirovic (ed.), *Brent Crude Oil*,
https://doi.org/10.1007/978-3-031-28232-4_8

111

the Brent market. Indeed, the two principal oil market PRAs, Platts and Argus, arguably owe much of their expansion in the latter part of the twentieth and early twenty-first centuries to the evolution of Brent, and to their ability to facilitate its existence.

Dawn of the Crude Oil Market

It's easy to forget that as recently as the 1970s, there was effectively no "market" for crude oil. In 1971, the price of West Texas Intermediate crude was \$2.71/bbl *for the entire year*—because prices were set by decree, either by oil majors or by OPEC producers. There was no particular reason to "trade" crude.

Neither Platts nor Argus—founded by Jan Nasmyth in 1970 as Europ-Oil Prices, and joined 14 years later by Adrian Binks, still the Argus CEO today—published a crude oil price report at the start of that decade; and these businesses were wholly focused on tracking activity in refined oil products markets in North America and Europe. That had been the entirety of Platts' business since 1923, when US journalist Warren Platt started up his *Oilgram Price Report*—a typewritten newssheet, distributed by hand in New York City.

Then came the UK's tax rule changes of the 1970s,[1] the US government's de-control of crude prices in 1981, the launch of the NYMEX crude futures contract in 1983, OPEC's tearful farewell to fixed pricing in 1986, and the eventually successful 1988 launch of IPE Brent futures.

Alongside that, the shock of the 1973 Arab Oil embargo led many of the international oil companies to start exploiting higher cost oil reserves in non-OPEC areas more intensively, particularly those in the North Sea and Alaskan North Slope. Companies such as BP, Exxon, and Shell were at the forefront of these developments, with BP the first to land Forties crude in the UK in 1975.

While the American oil companies—Exxon, Mobil, Chevron, Gulf, and Texaco—continued to produce and lift oil from OPEC members after the latter nationalised their oil fields, BP was in a more difficult position.

The Iranian revolution of 1979 meant that BP lost its favoured position in Iran and in the same year lost its access to Nigerian production. In 1980, BP expanded its supply department to start actually *trading* crude oil, initially focusing on Forties. But by the mid-1980s the light sweet Brent blend, produced by Shell and Exxon, started to dominate trading, and became an increasing focus for price reporters.

The price reporters leapt upon this new market. Argus launched its crude coverage in a twice a week report in 1976, while Platts launched its *Crude Oil MarketWire* in 1978. Argus followed suit with the daily *Argus Telex* a year later. In 1987, Platts and Argus began reporting the price of Dated Brent, and the rest—to some extent—is history.

THE TROUBLE WITH CRUDE OIL

However, all crude oil streams are finite, and extraction depletes reserves. It is in the nature of crude streams from single oil fields that their production eventually drops to an uneconomic level.

And from the perspective of a PRA accustomed to markets that consumed a seemingly never-interrupted supply of refined oil products, this was a bit of a problem as the Brent field production declined.

"Benchmark" prices in commodities markets arise by a curious accretive process in which broad marketplace agreement to use a particular price as a proxy for market value develops only under specific circumstances, and often very slowly. Those specific circumstances include *reliability of supply*, and *multiplicity of ownership*. No one wants to tie a long-term contract to a price for something that may unpredictably cease to exist, or something produced by a lone actor who may decide arbitrarily to change the volume, impose destination restrictions, or otherwise interfere with the spot value of the commodity.

That is why, after all, the primary benchmarks for *oil products* are almost exclusively prices for products produced in large refining hubs—Houston, Rotterdam, Singapore. Because in these places it doesn't matter if a refinery breaks down, or even explodes. There are backups.

Not so in the case of crude oil streams. This is stuff—and all slightly different stuff in terms of chemical composition, density, sulphur content, etc.—that comes out of the ground for a limited period of time only.

One has only to think of the fate of Alaska North Slope (ANS) crude, the mighty benchmark of North America in the 1980s, to appreciate that individual crude oil streams are at the mercy of multiple factors. Initially used by Saudi Arabia and its Gulf allies as the contract price benchmark for their crude exports to the US, ANS fell into disfavour with the big producing countries because it came to be controlled in effect by a single oil company—BP. As a result, in the early 1990s the pricing team at Saudi Aramco, under the guidance of their chief economist Laney Littlejohn (a former economics professor at Houston's Rice University), switched

Aramco's price benchmark for US sales to West Texas Intermediate (WTI).

The longevity of the WTI market is due in large measure to the fact that the crude involved is, and always has been, a blend of physical material fed to the Cushing, Oklahoma, hub—and latterly Midland, Texas—from multiple parts of the US. Everything "counts" as WTI, provided it meets the API gravity and sulphur content specifications.[2] And the grade, now a major export crude, benefits as such from starting life as an onshore pipeline crude that is readily mixed from an inherently connected system.

Not so Brent, which by its very nature flows from *unconnected* subsea oilfields in one of the world's more hostile production environments.

That a small cluster of wells 186 km northeast of the northernmost islands of Scotland, the Shetlands, should produce a crude oil that has become the "ultimate super-benchmark", is a phenomenon that repays much study. At its inception in 1976, Brent was merely one of the higher-producing fields in the North Sea.

Unintended Consequences of Tax Rules

But the adoption the previous year of new British tax rules under the UK government's Oil Taxation Act inadvertently propelled Brent to the status of one of the most actively traded crude oils in the world. The UK's Petroleum Revenue Tax (abolished in effect in 2016) was a 50% tax on oil producers' profits. But its complex rules allowed producers to declare, for taxation purposes, the *lowest price* achieved in a single one-month period in the spot sale of crude oil cargoes.

This rule was originally single-handedly responsible for so-called "tax-spinning"[3] among oil companies and trading houses: the practise of selling, re-buying, and re-selling a single cargo of crude oil multiple times. Trading and re-trading of theoretical "forward month" Brent cargoes occurred frenetically in the run-up to the moment each month when a piece of paper representing a cargo became a real physical cargo—the issuance by Shell of a loading programme for the coming weeks, with dates attached to each cargo.

At the moment that cargoes became physical, with loading dates, so-called "Dated Brent", the game of musical chairs would stop. Whoever was left holding the piece of paper with the official cargo nomination—and in the 1980s, it was literally a piece of paper: a telex—was then deemed the owner, and responsible for actually loading the cargo onto a ship.

Because each cargo of Brent could trade dozens of times in the run-up to this moment, tax-spinning inflated the notional volume of Brent to a massive extent. By 1982, production from the field had ramped up to 504,000 b/d—not bad for a couple of fields (technically Brent was a mix of Brent and Ninian crude oils[4]), but not an earth-shattering volume. But that physical volume was in effect multiplied to traded volume equivalent to the output of some of the largest OPEC producers of the age: Iran, Iraq, Kuwait, and at times to volumes equivalent to the Saudi Arabian production at the time of 4–5 million barrels a day (mbd).

PRAs—Volume, Transparency, and the Dawn of Real-Time Assessments

PRAs benefited greatly from this surge in observable trade, because it meant that price assessments derived from the Brent market were underpinned by large and increasingly transparent volumes of trade.

Both Platts and Argus found in the 1980s that there was little resistance from market participants to publishing the names of parties to transactions in this market, in stark contrast to other oil markets—and many other commodities markets: fertilizers and chemicals, for example—where, for decades, traders had insisted on confidentiality in exchange for communicating their market activity to journalists.

The publication of names further strengthened the transparency of the market, lending confidence to markets that the numbers published represented the real transactable value of North Sea crude. Moreover, as early as 1984, Platts launched one of the first real-time screen price services in commodities markets, called *Platts Global Alert*.

The service, initially distributed on a "green screen" via a McGraw-Hill dial-up computer service named EMIS, and via a small satellite distributor in Utah, included a page—known as "Page 3"[5]—on which the company began listing the transactions it unearthed in the crude oil market as a whole.

Back then, market reporting was strictly a telephone-based activity. John Kingston from Platts, who rose to head up oil reporting for the company a decade later—recalls how market information was obtained through dozens of hours a week of calling traders and brokers, discussing the market with them, collating the information gathered, and analysing it to make sense of it.

At Argus the Brent market was covered by Ray Payne, a former trader at Gulf Oil who followed a similar process to Kingston. Deals were not "submitted" (as some regulators fondly imagine)—they all had to be discovered. Bids and offers were not electronic but voice-brokered. There was no anchoring forward or futures contract as a reference point.[6]

As a result, the innocuous innovation by Platts *of putting crude prices on a screen* had an effect that in today's electronicised world is perhaps difficult to appreciate. It mushroomed in the 1990s into a service that had traders glued to their screens—as updates to the page became more and more real-time. It evolved into a bulletin board through which ongoing activity in crude markets was communicated, and ultimately into what is now named the "eWindow". Distribution of the service moved onto Reuters, Bloomberg, and multiple other data vendors as the world turned increasingly electronic on the eve of the birth of the Internet.

Critical to the success of "Page 3" was the fact that it was editorially moderated. Bids, offers, and deals only appeared on the page if they were deemed credible by Platts' editors. There was at the time no direct access by the market itself. That had the welcome effect of ensuring the page was not being "gamed" by traders engaging in spoof bids and offers, for example.

Out of the process developed a virtuous circle, in which the provision of near-real-time information on the market-built confidence in the marketplace itself to bid, offer, and trade around the visible numbers, which in turn created an ever-increasing flow of market information.

The success of "Page 3" was due also to the market measurement methodology the PRAs gradually adopted between the 1980s and 2001: namely to measure the price at a single "market on close" point in time. Decried by some as "game show pricing" the approach had the side-effect of making it possible to sell or buy a cargo at the exact price for that day—by delaying a transaction until the last possible moment. This was attractive to some players, regardless of whether or not the price was representative of the market as a whole at that specific instant in time. And indeed, there emerged market participants who took on responsibility for selling or buying at the close on behalf of others.

It also worked to boost Dated Brent as a benchmark, primarily because of the specific characteristics of how that market worked. Platts' attempts to replicate the "market on close" approach in other markets since 2002 have had, at best, mixed results, largely because market mechanics vary across different markets. European gasoline wholesale markets (2002) and US crude pipeline markets (2006) both switched to using Argus prices rather than accept an MOC approach. The European gasoline market, indeed, has if anything become a "market on open" with the majority of activity taking place in the first hour of the day's trading. The transparency of the Brent market attracted a great deal of interest from crude oil producers worldwide, and beginning in 1986, large producers in OPEC began tying their contract prices for crude oil exports to the European region to Brent. At the same time, trade in multiple other European and West African grades of crude oil became increasingly linked to Brent through spread trading, to the point where most, if not all, grades in these two regions began trading not in terms of outright prices but in terms of the differential to Dated Brent.

It became habitual to trade Nigerian crude, for example, as "Dated Brent plus" (or "minus"). It became a key part of the global crude complex to trade "Brent-Dubai"—a mechanism for physical exchange of cargoes, in which a single differential-based transaction enabled a trader to shift their geographical longs and shorts around the world, from North Sea to Middle East, or vice-versa, without going to the trouble of executing two transactions, one in Brent and one in Dubai crude. Brent-Dubai, though, also had the long-term effect of making Dubai effectively another crude whose value was in a sense derivative of Brent.

On top of that, the "dated"[7] nature of "Dated Brent" made it essentially unique among tradeable crude grades at the time. A "dated" market does not expire. There is no caesura between one month and the next, and no moment of expiry, because cargoes are always traded for loading X days forward. In the early days it was 7–21 days forward, but market pressure (and shortage of real cargoes) led to a gradual expansion of the loading window to the point where today it is 10 days to a month ahead.

This means the Dated Brent market, unlike monthly grades such as the Middle East's Oman or Dubai, creates a continuous time series that is hugely useful to traders seeking to hedge price risk in smaller increments than months.

As a result, a highly active market in Dated Brent swaps (technically contracts for difference, or CFDs) began to develop in the 1990s. The rise of the swaps market also got a shot in the arm from a January 1989 decision by the US Commodities and Futures Trading Commission *not to include* oil swaps (or gold) in the list of financial instruments over which it held sway. Banks and other swaps writers were free to offer them without CFTC oversight.[8] So, traders started using the swaps market to close the gap between the continuously "sliding window" of the Dated Brent price, and the monthly futures price as traded on the IPE exchange in London (later bought by the Intercontinental Exchange). In effect, it became possible to trade and hedge Dated Brent more precisely and farther along the time curve.

The swaps market acted to more closely connect physical Brent with futures to the point where, arguably, the futures market was in effect determining at what level it was possible to trade physical barrels.

The influence of Brent eventually spread globally. It has for example become a component in government pricing formulae for road fuels as far afield as China and Australia.

Evolving Methodologies

The closing methodologies that both Platts and Argus use for Brent today were unheard of in oil markets in the 1980s, when "value" was typically seen in markets as an "all day" affair from which a typical price might be extracted. Many non-energy commodities markets—fertilizers, petrochemicals, many metals—and indeed numerous sections of energy markets such as LNG, biomass, or coal still operate on that basis today.

But the use of a market close arose gradually. Increased deal flow in the early days of Brent made it possible to measure the market with increasing accuracy. A reliable number of deals in each trading period meant for the first time that a volume-weighted average (VWA) price carried actual meaning. Embraced by many market participants as a "fair" mechanism for representing their collective participation in a market, the VWA has become a staple of multiple commodities markets, from European gasoline to US crude oil.

The PRAs also used VWAs for Brent in the first years of rising liquidity in the market. But they found that the volume of trade, and the pattern of trade over the course of the trading day, increasingly meant that transaction volume was concentrated at the close of day in European markets.

On the final day each month before the announcement of the Dated Brent loading schedule, frenetic trading would occur immediately prior to 5 p.m., which was deemed the moment in time after which no further title transfer to a cargo could occur.

As a result, trades naturally began to cluster late in the day, and market activity earlier in the day became increasingly irrelevant.

Platts began measuring its averages first over a 30-minute end-of-day period in the run-up to 2 p.m. New York time (Platts, then part of US publishing house McGraw-Hill—now S&P Global, was at this time still assessing Brent from its New York office). The 30 minutes was then cut to 15, then to five, until at the end of the 1990s, there was a move to a "single point in time" definition of its published price for Brent. This "market on close" price was defined as the transactable value of Dated Brent, and other forward month Brents, at precisely 5 p.m. UK time—a close later moved to 4.30 p.m. But the methodology took into account market developments—bids, offers, and deals—for the whole of the 30-minute period prior to the close, creating an evolving picture of bids and offers that finished, typically, in a flurry of transactions.

Argus' methodology for its competing "North Sea Dated" price is virtually identical but uses a one-minute average of prices for forward Brent (whole month Brent) in the 60 seconds prior to 4.30 p.m., instead of a single point in time. The difference is minimal.

It is in the nature of market measurement methodology that, where the resulting price is used as a benchmark, *the methodology itself* has an impact on how markets trade. The gradual shift to a "final moment of play" concentrated market activity still more heavily at the end of the day, because market participants wanted to make sure that "their deal counted" in formulating the final price.

Brent Starts to Run Out
and the Birth of "Pool Pricing"

At the same time as all this was going on, however, the market was starting to develop a physical problem. Quite simply, the Brent field was running out.[9]

The number of dated cargoes in the Shell loading programme had begun declining in the late 1980s, and by 1994 had halved from the peak. From 1996 onwards, oil output went into steep decline and fell below 40,000 barrels a day in 1998. This naturally hugely reduced the number of cargoes available per month and led to sharply increased volatility in the Dated Brent price. It became financially feasible for market participants to "squeeze" the market by acquiring a disproportionate number of cargoes, locking them up, and pushing the price dramatically higher.

Large Middle Eastern oil producing countries, which had tied their contract prices for crude cargoes exported to Europe to the Brent price beginning in 1986, began to complain vociferously, and with increasing frequency, that the price was increasingly unrepresentative of market fundamentals. Similar voices began to be raised among US producers and European oil majors.

The market was "broken", ran the complaint. It was too easy for traders to buy up cargoes and push the price around without actually violating any regulatory rules.

North Sea producers scratched their heads to fix the problem. Would it be possible, for example, to physically connect the Brent field system to others by pipeline to boost the volume of production? If so, at what cost, given the enormous water depth of the North Sea?

In the event, the problem was solved by an innovative approach to price assessment, developed with the encouragement of Shell, BP, and others. The essential change was to reimagine a benchmark as a generic instrument rather than the value of a barrel of crude of a particular type.

The Argus North Sea Reference Price was an early attempt to solve the supply problem. Launched in 1999, this took a fixed proportion weighted average of the prices of a basket of North Sea crudes from UK and Norwegian waters: Forties, Flotta, Ekofisk, Oseberg, and Statfjord, as well as Brent itself.

But a weighted average is difficult to hedge—and might have the unwanted side-effect of involving market participants in having to try to trade all its components.

The preferred approach that emerged, therefore, and was then in fact implemented by Platts, was to "deem" other crude grades to be substitutes for Brent, to track the market for each, and to set the "Dated Brent" price at the <u>lowest</u> price being traded across the pool of crude.

This solution was similar to the one adopted for Dubai crude as it started to dry up in the late 1990s—namely to allow the *physical* delivery of an Oman cargo in place of a Dubai one. The difference in the case of Brent was the realisation that *virtual* substitution was all that was needed.

The effect of this "lowest price sets the benchmark" approach was to render pointless any attempt to squeeze the market upwards. If a single player bought all the available Brent cargoes, Brent's price would rise above the other grades in the pool and would no longer be the crude setting the price. The overall pool of cargoes would be so great that no single interest could take control of the market. The same would hold true of a squeeze on any of the other grades in the pool.

Thus, was born the price methodology known as "Brent Forties Oseberg (BFO)" which, beginning in 2002, first incorporated additional crude grades into "Brent" by virtual means. The term "Dated Brent" persisted, however, because it was written into contracts all over the world that market participants were reluctant to renegotiate. But "Brent" came to mean the broader North Sea crude price discovery complex.

BFO became BFOE, as Ekofisk crude joined the pool in 2007, and eventually BFOET, with the addition of Troll a decade later. The addition of Norwegian crudes symbolised in a sense a new market pragmatism, since by allowing their inclusion, traders were in effect ignoring Norway's history of state intervention in (or direct control of) the country's production levels—typically a no–no for any benchmark to stand a chance of getting off the ground.

The BFOET mechanism in theory was infinitely extensible, provided that comparable grades of crude oil continued to be available. And even less comparable grades, it turned out, could work. Sulphur content in Forties crude, for example, became increasingly a problem with the addition of output from the Buzzard field to the Forties blend in early 2007. Briefly, Platts dropped Forties from its BFO basket on the grounds that it was no longer a light sweet crude, causing market outcry and a flurry of trading activity using Argus North Sea Dated instead of Platts Dated Brent, and highlighting the difficulty of making changes to benchmarks without lengthy consultation and warning.

The situation was resolved when BP proposed the adoption of the concept by PRAs of a "sulphur de-escalator" by which buyers are compensated if crude once loaded and tested is found to contain sulphur above a certain threshold. This allows market participants to trade Forties as if it were comparable with the rest of the pool.

While the concept of pool pricing curbed upward price spikes and boosted the amount of oil available for benchmark inclusion, changes to tax rules again had an inadvertent effect on the market around this time.

In 2006, the UK government changed the tax rule that had hastened the growth of the Brent market in its infancy, with a belated recognition of the importance of PRAs.[10] The new taxation formula used an average of PRA assessments from Argus, Platts and a third price reporting agency, ICIS, to value the North Sea crudes—rather than the lowest price declared by a producer. This removed some of the incentive to trade each cargo multiple times and accelerated a decline in trading activity that has accompanied the fall in North Sea crude production.

Some Middle East producers had already had enough of Dated Brent by the time BFO was invented. In 2000, Saudi Aramco switched its European contract pricing to an average price derived from two months' worth of the IPE Brent futures markets—a move that arguably rebounded on Aramco, because the incorporation of the time structure of forward prices in its formulae meant its market experts were constantly adjusting premia and discounts to the "marker", not just for quality, but for time value, in order to keep its crude competitive. A few years later, in 2009, Aramco also dropped WTI from its export formula for the US, switching instead to an Argus price known as "ASCI"—the Argus Sour Crude Index, a volume-weighted average price whose makeup more closely reflects the quality of Saudi crude.

Riyadh's competitors in the Mideast Gulf virtually all followed suit. The departure of key producers as users of Dated Brent and WTI, however, had little effect on the broader popularity of the two benchmarks, which has continued to spread for the past two decades.

The price of Malaysia's Tapis crude—a key benchmark for light sweet values in Asia–Pacific—was for example supplanted by Dated Brent in 2008 as Tapis succumbed to a crisis of liquidity that drained market confidence.

Regulators Take an Interest

The 2008 financial crisis led to a greater government focus on systemic market risks. Inevitably commodities and the role of price reporting came under scrutiny. The G20,[11] through the International Organisation of Securities Commissions Committee 7 (or IOSCO),[12] started to examine the role of PRAs in the reporting of commodity markets and the creation of benchmarks used to settle financial derivative instruments. Committee 7 was assisted by representatives from OPEC, the International Energy Agency (IEA), and the International Energy Forum.

Over the years the large price reporting organisations, Argus, Platts, Opis, ICIS, Fastmarkets, and CRU, had professionalised the way they assessed markets and developed rigorous codes of conduct that included editorial matters, the separation of commercial discussions from price reporting and prohibition of investments in companies that traded commodities that the PRA reported.

The similarity of approach between different PRAs is at first sight striking. But much is perhaps explained by the fact that almost without exception, newcomers to the PRA space—in energy at least—have been founded by journalists who spotted an emerging market opportunity while working for an existing price reporting service. Lookalike replication of existing coverage by newcomers rarely works—first mover advantage is a powerful force in market reporting, and as already noted, it takes serious market dissatisfaction to bring about a change in benchmark use. As a result, successful new PRAs tend to operate in new market spaces, while preserving the tested reporting ethics of their competitors. ICIS for instance was founded in 1980 by Humphrey Hinshelwood, a former Platts reporter, as "Independent Chemical Information Service" and later rebranded with the same initials "Independent Commodity Intelligence Services" after its acquisition by RELX.[13] Gas market specialist Heren Energy, acquired by ICIS in 2008, was founded by Patrick Heren, former editor of World Gas Intelligence, part of the Energy Intelligence group. (More recent entrants to the PRA field, like Quantum Commodity Intelligence, or General Index, have also been founded by PRA alumni.)

The codes of conduct these businesses have universally come to recognise as vital for their existence, because they underpin market trust in the prices they publish, now became the basis of IOSCO's Principles for Oil Price Reporting Agencies (PRA Principles), which were agreed in October 2012 after intensive work involving Committee 7 members led by the US Commodity Futures Trading Commission and the UK Financial Services Authority, and the PRAs.

In November 2012, the G20 endorsed IOSCO's PRA Principles as the standard for the creation of commodity benchmarks used to settle derivative financial contracts. In 2016, the IOSCO PRA Principles were incorporated by the EU into Annexe 2 of the Benchmark Regulation for the settlement of financial commodity derivatives in Europe.

TWENTY YEARS ON

In the intervening years, more pricing has migrated away from Dated Brent to Brent futures: the key regional import market of China's Shandong province tends for instance to buy its imported cargoes from sources as diverse as Brazil, Congo (Brazzaville), and Russia at differentials to ICE Brent.

But the biggest challenge to the benchmark has come from without. The shale revolution and the lifting of the US crude export ban saw the emergence of a large, market-based export stream that was quickly accepted as a baseload crude by European and global refiners. Once unique as a large, openly traded light sweet "complex", Brent now had a challenger in the form of US Gulf Coast exports of Midland-quality WTI.

At the same time, since 2018 the problem of physical supply for Brent has reared its head again. This time, there is no ready answer in terms of local North Sea crudes, and users of Brent are again facing the question of whether there is "an exit", or a more representative, reliable benchmark for their needs.

Dated Brent itself has become an increasingly byzantine construct. Computing the price, for Platts, Argus, and ICIS alike, involves first generating a closing price for ICE Brent futures, then subtracting from or adding to that a swap differential value representing the midpoint day of the forward Dated time window (10 days to a month ahead), and then further adjusting by the traded value (also a differential) of the lowest valued member of the BFOET pool, the least liquid component of the process. This multi-step process reflects how the market trades. Swaps trade as a differential to futures, BFOET trades as a differential to swaps, so to derive a fixed price number, the market process needs to be followed.

Purists might argue that this is the "tail wagging the dog", or a "circular market" since futures markets are supposed to exist to hedge physical risk. And the complexity of how the many Brents—dated, forward physical, futures, swaps—interact has only contributed to the sense that change may be needed.

For some years, the market has wrestled with the idea of somehow incorporating delivered crude oil into the northwest European pricing mechanism—that is, crude of comparable quality entering the market from elsewhere. In October 2018, Argus launched prices on a delivered Rotterdam basis for several grades of light sweet crude including WTI, Azeri BTC Blend, Algerian Saharan Blend, and Nigerian Bonny Light, Qua Iboe and Escravos.

A TRANSATLANTIC MERGER

Shortly afterwards, in February 2019, Argus launched a version of Dated Brent called New North Sea Dated, which incorporated prices of the above delivered grades, adjusted to align pricing terms with the BFOET grades.

Over time it became clear, however, that WTI was the most regularly delivered and transparently traded of the extraneous crudes, and thus the most appropriate addition to the pool. On its own, indeed, it arguably renders the other grades superfluous.

Market opinion has thus coalesced around the concept of adding delivered WTI to the BFOET crude pool. The sheer volume of WTI crude making its way to Europe—around 1.14 mn b/d in 2022—makes a compelling argument for its use as part of the pricing mechanism. The five crudes in the BFOET pool, by contrast, make up only around 670,000 b/d.

As a result, both Platts and Argus are preparing to update their North Sea benchmark indexes to include WTI, and Shell rewrote its Brent contract in 2022 to permit the delivery into forward Brent positions of WTI cargoes from specific terminals nominated by both Argus and Platts. With effect from May 2023, Argus' primary North Sea Dated assessment will include Midland WTI cargoes from any of 12 US Gulf terminals. Platts has taken a similar approach and will launch its own version of the price for cargoes delivered from June 2023 onwards.

The change will mean that in addition to the five BFOET grades, a seller can nominate a WTI cargo meeting the specifications laid down by the two PRAs for delivery into a "Brent" trade.

This will be the biggest change to the North Sea crude benchmark—and thus the whole Brent pricing complex—since its inception. It is a remarkable vote of confidence in WTI by the conservative Brent market, just six years after the export ban on WTI was lifted in the last days of the Obama administration. But just a few months ahead of implementation by the PRAs, critical questions remain around how this method will actually work.

The unique strengths of WTI—its broad participation (30–40 unique participants) and un-matched optionality (storage, domestic refining, export to any region around the world)—present specific challenges for shoe-horning it into the North Sea complex. With sellers retaining commercial optionality up until the time of title transfer, it becomes impossible to introduce the loading programmes enjoyed in the North Sea, thus rendering it impossible to regulate the flow of US-origin crude into Europe.

What the impact of the addition of WTI to Brent is likely to be remained unclear and could include freight adjustments to the price to "handicap" the blend's impact on the European benchmark. At all events, the data to date suggests that WTI will not simply be another floating cap on the Brent price, but a key determinant.

Under the "lowest of" methodology, had WTI been included in the BFOET basket, it would have set the benchmark on half of the working days from February 2019 until the end of 2022, and would have resulted in a price on average 70 cents/barrel lower than the BFOET only method.[14] Some observers argue that once a crude becomes a benchmark it gains a premium and that WTI's impact could be less pronounced in future, but the historical data is currently the market's only guide.

If WTI becomes the default Brent benchmark setting grade, it raises further questions about what the Brent price will represent. Over the past 40 years, Brent has evolved to become a sophisticated instrument for the pricing of North Sea crude as well as those crudes it is competing with globally.

WTI too has accumulated a constellation of derivatives and related prices around it, not least the robust pipeline markets at Midland and Houston where the volume of trade and diversity of participation now dwarfs anything in the physical North Sea market. The WTI Houston and Midland physical markets have around 30–40 unique participants in a given month with around 800,000–1 million b/d of trade at each location as of late 2022, representing dozens of deals each day. By contrast, the North Sea BFOET physical cargo market in the same period had only around five deals per month and a similar number of unique participants, adding up to only around 100,000 b/d of trade.

But the Brent-WTI spread has been one of the closest watched indicators in the oil market, allocating flows either to North America or to Europe or Asia, where Brent pricing has become the standard. What does it mean if the same crude is setting benchmark prices at both ends of the spread? Will Brent simply become a derivative of the WTI market as Dubai arguably became of Brent: the price of WTI at the US Gulf coast plus the cost of freight to Rotterdam?

One of the crutches of the Brent market, moreover, was the large volume of Russian Urals crude that was delivered into European refining centres and priced at differentials to Dated Brent. But most of that crude has been excluded from the region since the EU implemented its embargo in December 2022, leaving the physical Brent market looking thinner and more exposed.

The PRAs hold up a mirror to the market, but in their unique independent and competitive position as benchmark providers, they can also usher in change. The addition of WTI to Brent by the leading PRAs, and the market's acceptance of this change, is a sign that the grand old European benchmark is succumbing to the gravitational pull of the resurgent US export market.

NOTES

1. See the chapter by Liz Bosley.
2. Since, CME has introduced some additional quality specifications. See: https://www.cmegroup.com/content/dam/cmegroup/rulebook/NYMEX/2/200.pdf.
3. For details on "tax spinning", see the chapter by Liz Bosley.
4. On co-mingling the two, see the chapter by Colin Bryce.
5. For an example of a trader following the information from the "page 3", see the chapter by Kurt Chapman.
6. The cargoes were trading at say, $18 a barrel, as opposed to the first forward or futures month Brent plus or minus a differential say, the first forward month was $17 plus a premium of $1 a barrel. Note that both approaches would result in the same, fixed price deals.
7. For explanation how Brent becomes Dated, see the chapter by David Godfrey.
8. *New York Times*, January 6, 1989: https://www.nytimes.com/1989/01/06/business/exemptions-by-the-cftc.html.
9. This does not necessarily mean that there is no physical oil left in the field, but that it is not economically viable to exploit it (given the prevailing technology and prices).
10. https://www.legislation.gov.uk/ukdsi/2006/0110753453/introduction, with reference to PRAs here: https://www.legislation.gov.uk/ukdsi/2006/0110753453/regulation/4?view=plain.
11. Group of Twenty is an intergovernmental forum comprising 19 countries and the European Union (EU).
12. https://www.iosco.org/about/?subsection=display_committee&cmtid=18#:~:text=Committee%207%20focuses%20on%20issues,OTC%20derivatives%2C%20and%20commodity%20derivatives.

13. https://www.icis.com/explore/?cmpid=PSC%7CICIS%7C2022-EURO%
    7Ccompetitors&sfid=7014G000000j6CgQAI&gclid=Cj0KCQiA_bieBhD
    SARIsADU4zLcXjUxNmwor8KIwHyddUvfMH6xROfOcxwXAD525aC
    Wgzx37YDB9LRMaAniiEALw_wcB.
14. This calculation is based on the performance of Argus' "New North Sea
    Dated" price, as published in the Argus Crude report since February
    2019, which includes WTI as well as the BFOET crudes.

CHAPTER 9

Crossroads: Past, Present and Future of Brent

Adi Imsirovic

Abstract Brent may well be becoming terribly complex, but the Brent market naturally evolved over time, and its complexity and even some redundancies are natural features, not dissimilar from the features of the human body—they are not always pretty or perfect, but they work well. The inclusion of WTI in the Brent contract is a step in the right direction. If executed carefully, it should not only massively increase the volume of oil underpinning the contract, but it should also bring the mighty WTI benchmark closer to Brent. As the US production continues to grow in foreseeable future, supplying the whole world without destination and other restrictions, the inclusion of WTI is a long-term solution for the Brent benchmark.

Keywords Brent · Complexity · Market instruments · WTI midland · Benchmarks

A. Imsirovic (✉)
Oxford Institute for Energy Studies, Ascot, UK
e-mail: adi.imsirovic@surreyenergy.uk

129

CROSSROADS—PRESENT

In 2023 the key global oil benchmark, Brent, stands at a crossroads. We are witnessing one of the greatest changes in its history, the inclusion of the West Texas Intermediate (WTI) Midland crude into its list of deliverable grades of oil into the Brent contract.[1]

The change has been preceded by years of discussions and consultations and has polarised the oil market. Was the inclusion of Johan Sverdrup unjustifiably rejected? Will a new benchmark work? Will WTI dominate the new benchmark? If so, why bother with Brent altogether and instead simply use the price of the dominant crude at the loading points in the US Gulf? The oil industry was definitely split by some of these questions. The authors of this book also had differing opinions.

'Might it finally be the case that Brent, on its colourful journey, lengthier even than the Odysseus from Troy, may not make it home?' wonders Colin Bryce.

'WTI Midland has legs of its own and does not need Brent' argues Liz Bossley, adding 'It would be considerably simpler to let Brent atrophy and for WTI and/or some other benchmark to take over by a process of evolution. But those parties with a vested interest, such as futures exchanges and PRAs, are going to extraordinary lengths to keep Brent alive'.[2]

While I am a lot more optimistic about the future of Brent, I cannot disagree with the fact that the industry has vested interests in keeping the benchmark alive. Many millions of barrels of forwards, futures and other various derivative contracts have been agreed on the basis of Brent price, way into the future. So, the industry desperately needs Brent to continue to function, and to function well, in a way that does not change values of those outstanding contracts. That is not an easy task.

PAST

So, what are the lessons of the economic history that we can learn from this book? For me, they are many, but a couple of lessons stand out:

All contracts face their crossroads at some stage. WTI had a fair share of problems, from the 1975 ban on US oil exports, the collapse in oil production in the US in the mid-1980s to the recent collapse in the price of the benchmark to almost –$40 a barrel.[3]

The oil price crash of WTI in 1986 had a dramatic effect on the domestic production, which fell by over 1.5 mbd and caused over 25,000 wells to be shut, many of them permanently. Total open interest in the WTI contract fell to less than 100,000 contracts, a fraction of the usual outstanding trades. Starved of the local crude oil supply, the inland refineries had to import foreign oil from the US Gulf, using reversed pipeline flows. Those imports became competitive and the New York Mercantile Exchange (NYMEX)[4] soon introduced an 'alternative delivery procedure', which allowed for the foreign sweet crudes to be delivered into the contract. This allowed for delivery of a number of light, sweet grades of oil, including Brent, Oseberg, Bonny Light, Qua Iboe and a few others. The impact of this measure was not only to improve liquidity, but also to increase the 'depth' of the market as more new players were able to deliver oil into the contract. Open interest in WTI took off and grew steadily to about half a million contracts in the 1990s.[5] The lesson from this episode is that there is no reason why the inclusion of WTI into the Brent contract should not be manageable.

Another lesson is that complexity is normal in the process of natural evolution of a benchmark. Any gradual evolution of markets, just as the biological evolution of human body, is full of compromises and imperfections. It is a '… cumulative process in which each stage is more useful than the one before'.[6] The human body is a good example of an imperfect system that evolved appendix, wisdom teeth and even the human eye. The same imperfections are true of all naturally evolved markets.

The fact that Brent has evolved a large number of instruments, collectively known to as the 'Brent complex' is a good thing. Each instrument has evolved to play an important role in facilitating trade and mitigating risk. For example, as oil markets became more volatile, the CFD market grew out of a need to convert fixed-price deals into floating Dated Brent-related prices (and the other way round). Later, CFD 'rolls' (buying one week of CFDs, while selling another) grew out of a need to shift Dated pricing from one week into another. The DFL market grew out of a need to hedge refinery margins, normally done on monthly basis and in relation to futures, rather than forward Brent market, and so on. By the same token, future evolution of Brent is likely to be gradual, and it may well involve some innovations in the WTI contract as well.[7]

However numerous and complex, all these instruments in the Brent market have evolved to serve a particular function in at a particular point in time. As a result, oil price shocks such as the price collapse in April 2020 (caused by the COVID-19 pandemic), had far less impact on Brent than on the other benchmarks.[8] The impact of the demand shock was absorbed by the price differentials to Dated Brent and then to Dated Brent itself, relative to forward and futures Brent markets. Only then, the spreads and the absolute price level came under pressure.[9] Brent behaved just as it was supposed to do. It passed the test of a severe price shock, a very reassuring sign for the international oil market.

THE FUTURE OF BRENT

The current Brent benchmark has taken decades to become what it is today. Underpinned by English law, standardised contracts, no destination restrictions, tax advantages for oil majors in 'spinning' the cargoes and volume tolerance advantages[10] for traders and for all those with large 'Brent books', the North Sea Brent market developed as the premiere, transparent and liquid spot market.

But trading is not a democratic process—it works on 'one dollar, one vote' basis. Like most markets, Brent has favoured large players, price-makers, who provided the liquidity of the contract. In return, those large players[11] dominated the market and made large trading profits.[12] For this reason, these companies have had vested interest in maintaining smooth functioning of Brent. From adding physical cargoes at the time of alleged squeezes[13] to amending their general terms and conditions[14] to accommodate changes to the contract, large players such as Shell and BP have played a pivotal role in the genesis and the development of the Brent market and will continue to do so in future. In the process, smaller players, the price-takers, have benefited from a stable benchmark, generally reflecting market fundamentals, and having a liquid tool for managing the oil price risk.

But if the large open interest of forward, futures and other derivative contracts is to remain unaffected by changes in the benchmark and if Brent is to remain the premiere international benchmark, there is no room for complacency. The whole market would have to step up and take part in shaping the contract.

The inclusion of WTI in the Brent contract is a step in the right direction. If executed carefully, it should not only massively increase the volume of oil underpinning the contract, but it should also bring the mighty WTI benchmark closer to Brent. As the US production continues to grow in foreseeable future, supplying the whole world without destination and other restrictions, the inclusion of WTI is a long-term solution for the Brent benchmark.

This is not to say that Brent will remain the most important global benchmark forever. The oil flows have already shifted, so that the centre of gravity of oil trade is already located 'east of Suez'. But the emerging benchmarks in the Persian Gulf and China are parochial and often subject to government intervention, making them unsuitable to become anything more than regional benchmarks.[15]

With that in mind, a word of caution is needed here. The recent COVID-19 pandemic and the Russian invasion of Ukraine have brought about increasing government intervention in energy markets everywhere, including the US, EU and the UK. Such interventions have often been poorly targeted,[16] and even included price caps for oil and gas markets.[17] Such measures could result in shortages of these vital sources of energy in the market.[18] At best, they may fragment markets and make it hard to trade energy.

In the energy sector, government policy is always the key to economic outcomes, and we can only hope that our leaders learn from economic history to which our book makes a modest contribution, and support rather than impede the workings of well-functioning markets such as Brent.

NOTES

1. There are two key contracts, Dated Brent, and forward Brent.
2. Both comments are from our private correspondence, published here with their permission.
3. See Imsirovic (2021), Chapter 13.
4. Later taken over by Chicago Mercantile Exchange or CME.
5. Ibid., p. 190.
6. Dawkins (1986), Chapter 3.
7. The inclusion of WTI Midland in the Brent contract means that the transparent Dated Brent forward curve may well result in a creation of a transparent WTI Midland FOB USG curve (and perhaps lead to a need to trade WTI CFD swaps).
8. See Fattouh and Imsirovic (2020).
9. Ibid., p. 7.
10. At least in the early decades of the contract. For details, see Chapter 5 of this book.
11. For market concentration in Brent, see Imsirovic (2021), p. 163.
12. See: https://www.reuters.com/business/energy/shell-makes-record-40-billion-annual-profit-2023-02-02/#:~:text=Shell%20also%20posted%20record%20fourth,of%20%2431%20billion%20in%202,008.

13. See Chapters 4 and 6 of this book.
14. Specifically, SUKO 1990, with further amendments.
15. In case of the Shanghai INE oil contract, see: Imsirovic and Meidan (2020). In case of IFAD Murban contract, see Imsirovic (March 2021). For Oman DME contract, see Imsirovic (2018).
16. Rather than using cash transfers to the needy, governments have resorted to blanket subsidies. This is likely to prolong energy crisis and slow down energy transition. See: https://theconversation.com/how-to-tackle-the-uk-cost-of-living-crisis-four-economists-have-their-say-188625.
17. G7 introduced price caps for Russian oil (December 2022) and petroleum products (February 5, 2023) as well as a price cap for gas (https://www.reuters.com/business/energy/eu-countries-make-final-push-gas-price-cap-deal-this-year-2022-12-19/).
18. For my views on these policies see: https://www.energyintel.com/00000183-5b0b-d675-afef-7f8b7d760000 and https://theconversation.com/green-transition-will-be-less-painful-if-we-avoid-repeating-1970s-policy-errors-in-the-oil-market-172193.

References

Dawkins R. (1986): 'The Blind Watchmaker', Penguin Books.

Fattouh B. and Imsirovic A. (2020): 'Oil Benchmarks Under Stress', Oxford Energy Comment, April 2020.

Imsirovic A. (2018): 'What Next for Asian Benchmarks?—A Footnote', OIES Energy Comment, November 2018.

Imsirovic A. (2021): 'Reassessing Murban IFAD Outlook', World Energy Opinion, Energy Intelligence, March 2021.

Imsirovic A. and Meidan M. (2020): 'The Shanghai Oil Futures Contract and the Oil Demand Shock', OIES China Energy Brief 16, July 2020.

INDEX

© The Editor(s) (if applicable) and The Author(s), under exclusive
license to Springer Nature Switzerland AG 2023
A. Imsirovic (ed.), *Brent Crude Oil*,
https://doi.org/10.1007/978-3-031-28232-4

Printed in the United States
by Baker & Taylor Publisher Services